Science Made Simple

Grade 4

Written by Diane Vardner
Illustrated by Don O'Connor

PHOTO CREDITS
page 3: Stopwatches photograph by Carlye Calvin
page 30: Rustling Cables photograph by Eric Wunrow
page 45: Gears photograph by Carlye Calvin
page 68: Water photograph by Eric Wunrow

FS-23214 Science Made Simple Grade 4
All rights reserved–Printed in the U.S.A.
Copyright © 1997 Frank Schaffer Publications
23740 Hawthorne Blvd.
Torrance, CA 90505

P9-BJQ-108

Introduction

Children have an inherent drive to find out about the world around them. They are curious about what they see or experience, and they often display their interest by asking questions.

What do animals eat?

Why do things fall down?

What causes rust?

Why is the ocean salty?

These and other questions are children's attempts to make sense of their environment.

Science is learned best by actively engaging in inquiries. That is the way scientists study the natural world and propose explanations based on evidence from their work. Inquiries work best when students develop knowledge and understanding by doing activities. The experiences in this book encourage students to seek answers by making observations; posing questions; examining books and other sources of information to find what is already known; planning experiments and variables; using tools to gather, analyze, and interpret data; proposing explanations and predictions; and communicating their results. As you involve your students in the various activities, there are suggested questions that help you guide your class through the learning process. In addition, this resource provides information on literature, bulletin boards, extensions into other curricular areas, and technology such as World Wide Web sites and instructional television (ITV).

Science Made Simple Grade 4 can be used alone or as a part of any science program. An introductory unit covers safety guidelines, the process of observation, the role of scientists, and the scientific method. The book is divided into three sections: Life Science (covering the topic of environment), Physical Science (covering the topics of actions and interactions and forces and motion), and Earth Science (covering the topic of oceanography).

Science is both product (words and facts) and process (the activities of scientists). It is hoped that as you implement the activities and suggestions in this book, your students will discover the process of science and become better observers and problem-solvers. Emphasis should be placed not on coming up with the right answers, but on doing science the right way. Science will become fun and meaningful as your students are prepared to make decisions they must make as adults—decisions that are increasingly dependent on a clear understanding of science.

FS-23214 Science Made Simple ▪ © Frank Schaffer Publications, Inc.

Science Safety Guidelines

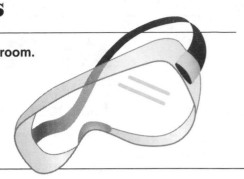

- While students remain seated, conduct a visual safety tour of your room.

- Point out the location of any safety equipment.

- Demonstrate how to properly use eye protection.

- Demonstrate how to properly note the odor of a chemical.

EXPLORATION
Class Activity

Allow each child to choose a science safety rule from page 2. Have each child draw the rule on a piece of unlined paper and write the rule on the back of the paper. Hold up a finished picture and see if other students can guess what the rule is. Play this guessing game several times with pictures that illustrate different rules. The first few times, children may need to look at the handout. After a while, they will know the rule without looking at the list.

SAFETY BULLETIN BOARD
Class Activity

Turn the students' pictures into a bulletin board. If there are children who speak other languages, you may want to translate the rules and post them along with the pictures and the rules in English.

AUDIOVISUAL EXTENSION
Group Activity

If you have access to a camcorder, have groups of children plan and record a presentation of the safety rules. Storyboarding is an excellent way to plan written material to be filmed on a video camcorder. Assign each group of three students a safety rule. Have them draw a large box on a sheet of paper for each line of narration they want to record, similar to a large cartoon strip. Tell the students to plan each scene they want to film inside a box using stick figures. Underneath each box, have them write the dialog that they will be speaking in the video. Tell students to plan what props they will need, what angles will be shot, and any special video effects such as fading out.

Science Safety Guidelines

The major causes of science laboratory accidents are inattention, carelessness, and unsafe behavior. Follow the safety guidelines below and your science time should be trouble-free.

Fire and Heat
- Tie back long hair or loose clothing when working with flames.
- If a fire starts, do not run or panic. Cover the area with a fire blanket. Notify the teacher.
- Look for all safety warnings before doing an activity.
- Do not touch hot glassware.
- Use caution with all hot liquids.

Eye Safety
- Wear eye protection when working with open flames or chemicals, or when doing any activity that could harm the eyes.
- Do not shine direct sunlight into the eyes with a magnifier or mirror.

Glassware
- Examine all glassware before using.
- Do not use broken or chipped glassware.

Neatness
- Keep your work area clear except for science materials.
- Clean up before leaving the class.
- Put away all materials where instructed.
- Do not throw chemicals into the sink unless instructed by the teacher.

Chemicals
- Never taste chemicals unless instructed to do so.
- Never directly smell any chemical. Instead wave the chemical in the air, directing the smell toward your nose.
- If any chemical is spilled, notify the teacher immediately.

Behavior
- Do not run or play in the laboratory.
- Notify the teacher of an accident or any broken equipment immediately.

Be Wise

Follow the Safety Guidelines

FS-23214 Science Made Simple ▪ © Frank Schaffer Publications, Inc.

The Powers of Observation

To observe is to use the evidence of our senses to obtain scientific information. Observations can be descriptive using words such as *hot, cold, shiny, dull, black, white, rough, or heavy.* Descriptive observations should not express opinions such as ugly, smelly, or pretty. Observations can be expressed in terms of numbers that reflect a measurement such as time, weight, distance, speed, or temperature.

The Powers of Observation on pages 4 and 5 involves learning to be good observers. A candle will be observed at three separate times. Each time the candle is observed, the groups will be asked to make two types of observations: one that uses descriptive words and one that uses numbers or measurements. The candle will be examined first unlit. Five descriptive and three numerical observations will be made. Have the children place the candle in the clay on the lid/cardboard and then light the candle. Try to avoid having drafts in the room. **Remember to explain safety rules pertaining to open flames.** If possible, turn off the lights for a minute so groups can observe the colors in the flame. Five descriptive and two numerical observations will be made. At a signal, instruct groups to gently blow out their candles and make final observations. Five descriptive and three numerical observations will be made.

SCIENCE IS . . .

Understanding the nature of science and its methods is necessary to appreciate how scientists work. Science is guided by principles that are testable, objective, and consistent. Scientists use observations, inferences, facts, hypotheses, and theories to predict and explain phenomena. Science is based on testable ideas. Reproduce page 6 for your students to keep in their notebooks as a reminder of the way scientists solve problems using the scientific method.

Class Activity

The Powers of Observation

Question:
Which type of observation, descriptive or numerative (involving numbers and measurement), is more reliable?

Prediction:
On your record sheet, predict how many observations you can make describing a birthday candle.

Materials:
birthday candle
clay
ruler
metal lid

Procedure:
1   Examine the candle using your five senses. On your record sheet, write five observations that describe the candle.
2. On your record sheet, write two observations of the candle that involve numbers or measurement. Examples may include length of wick, length and width of candle, or number of threads in the wick.
3. Place the clay on the center of the lid and put the base of the candle in the clay. Your teacher will light your candle. Remember to use caution around open flames.
4. On your record sheet, write five observations that describe and two observations that involve measurement. Do not burn the ruler or anything besides the candle.
5. When your teacher instructs you, gently blow out the candle. On your record sheet, write five observations that describe and three observations that involve measurements.

Results:
Record your observations on your record sheet.

Conclusion:
Answer the following question on your record sheet:
Which form of data, descriptive or numerative, do you think is more reliable? Why?

FS-23214 Science Made Simple ▪ © Frank Schaffer Publications, Inc.

The Powers of Observation

Question: Which type of observation, descriptive or numerative (involving numbers and measurement), is more reliable?

Prediction: How many observations can you make describing a birthday candle?

Results: Record your observations below.

Unlit Candle

Description
1. _____
2. _____
3. _____
4. _____
5. _____

Measurement
1. _____
2. _____

Lit Candle

Description
1. _____
2. _____
3. _____
4. _____
5. _____

Measurement
1. _____
2. _____

Candle After Burning

Description
1. _____
2. _____
3. _____
4. _____
5. _____

Measurement
1. _____
2. _____

Conclusion: Which form of data, descriptive or numerative, do you think is more reliable? Why? _____

_____

$\int$cience **I**s...

Who is a scientist?
A scientist is a person who is curious about the natural world.
Professional scientists are trained in certain techniques and methods.

What does a scientist do?
Scientists solve problems.
Scientists ask questions.
Scientists make observations.
Scientists gather information.
Scientists make predictions.
Scientists test their predictions.
Scientists keep data from their tests.
Scientists keep trying until they find the right answer.
Scientists communicate with others about their results.

What is the scientific method?
It is a way of thinking. Not all scientists use all of the steps, and the steps may sometimes be used out of order. These steps are also used by people who aren't scientists.

Step 1—State the problem, usually in the form of a question.
Step 2—Research what is already known.
Step 3—Give a hypothesis, or a possible answer, to the question based on the information you gathered.
Step 4—Test your hypothesis by doing an experiment and collecting observations in the form of data.
Step 5—Analyze or study your information collected from observations and experiments.
Step 6—Based on your collected and analyzed data, make a conclusion whether your hypothesis is correct or not. If it is incorrect, it must be changed and retested.
Step 7—Communicate with others what you found out. Other scientists need to know what has been done and what needs to still be studied. They may repeat the experiment to see if they get the same results. They may find ways to apply the findings to their own work.

FS-23214 Science Made Simple ▪ © Frank Schaffer Publications, Inc.

Life Science

Nature brings out children's sense of wonder. They observe the living things around them—the plants and animals—and visit places such as zoos, aquariums, and national parks. They hear and read words such as *endangered* and *extinct* and begin to ask why some animals and plants need to be protected. As they continue to make sense of how living things depend on each other, they will ask the much bigger question, "What role will I play in the future of living things on this planet?"

LITERATURE RESOURCES

These books are recommended as resources to help students learn about the environment.

The Great Kapok Tree by Lynne Cherry (Harcourt Brace, 1990). In this book, the many different animals that live in a great kapok tree in the Brazilian rain forest try to convince a man with an ax of the importance of not cutting down their home.

In the Woods by Ermanno Cristini and Luigi Puricelli (Scholastic, 1983). Illustrations present a wordless panorama of the woods where a variety of insects, birds, plants, and animals share a habitat. Other titles include *In the Pond* and *In My Garden*.

Everglades by Jean Craighead George (HarperCollins, 1995). The author of *Julie of the Wolves* describes the evolution of this unique area and the impact humans have had on its once abundant life.

One Small Square—Woods by Donald Silver (W.H. Freeman, 1995). The author explains how to investigate the plant and animal life found in a small section of the woods. Other titles include *Seashore, Cave, Backyard, African Savanna, Arctic Tundra, Pond,* and *Cactus Desert*.

Food Webs

Animals eat plants and in turn are often eaten by other animals. This is called a *food chain*. The connection of many food chains is called a *food web*. As you give your class an opportunity to explore a food web that exists in a marine environment, your students will begin to see that changes in one part of the food web will affect the entire food web.

A FOOD WEB

Class Experiment

Materials: set of Role Cards (pages 13–16), several balls of yarn, scissors, copies of pages 10–11, *Food Roles* sheet (page 12), set of Role Cards, large sheet of paper, ruler, pencil

Exploration: Give each student a Role Card. Explain that this will be the animal or plant that he or she will pretend to be. Have the students read their cards to find out what their organisms eat. Take the students outside and form a circle. As the students read aloud what they eat, the children who have the cards with the matching organisms will raise their hands. Assign anyone without a card to be a helper. Helpers will give one end of the yarn to the student who reads the card and the other end to whomever they eat. This can be achieved by the helper passing the ball of yarn and cutting it when the "food" is holding the ball. (The yarn is the symbol of energy passing along in the form of food.) Anyone who eats more than one organism will share yarn with more than one classmate. Make sure that the circle remains the same size throughout the activity. As the students read aloud what they eat and their "food" connects with them by the yarn, a very large web will form. Helpers will have to bend down to go under the web as it gets larger. Once each child has read his or her card, ask your class what might happen if an oil spill occurred and killed all the phytoplankton. (*Everything will be affected.*) Cut the strings of the phytoplankton to symbolize that it is dead. All animals that eat the phytoplankton will now die and their strings need to be cut. Continue cutting the strings until all animals are dead.

Next, return to the classroom and give each group a *Food Roles* sheet. Explain to your class that all living things have a role in the ecosystem. *Producers* make their own food and are usually green plants. *Consumers* have to eat another organism. *Predators* are animals that eat other living animals. *Prey* are the animals that are eaten. *Decomposers* eat the remains and wastes of dead plants and animals.

For a follow-up activity, give each group a complete set of Role Card sheets, a large sheet of paper, and the *Food Webs* student pages. Tell the students that they are going to draw the food web that they made outside on paper by drawing a large circle and writing the names of each animal from the Role Cards on the edges of the circle. Have them draw arrows connecting animals to their food. Once they have made their food web on paper, have them complete the record sheet.

Discovery: Certain organisms serve as predator or prey for many animals. The food web is a visual reminder of the interconnections in the ecosystem and that removing a member or destroying the home of one part of the food web can cause the entire web to fall apart.

FOOD WEB BULLETIN BOARD

Have each student research what his or her animal looks like using animal books or encyclopedias. Let students draw the animals and color them. Children who have microscopic animals such as the phytoplankton and zooplankton can make a picture of a magnifying glass and the organisms seen through it. Place the pictures on the bulletin board and connect the animals and what they eat using yarn.

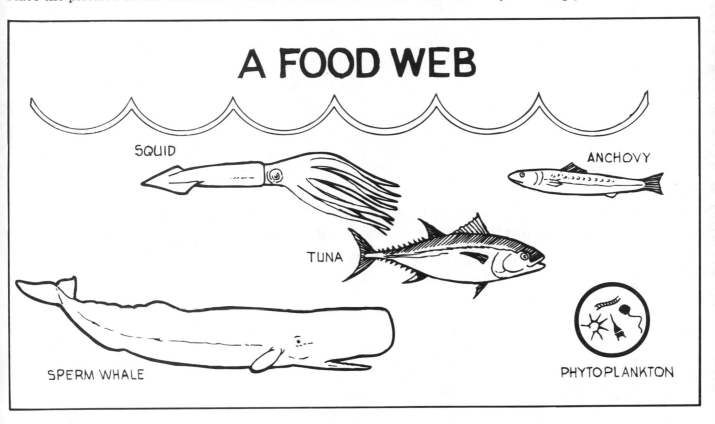

FAMOUS ENVIRONMENTALISTS

Have your students research the following famous environmentalists:

Rachel Carson—Her book *Silent Spring* showed the world the danger of widespread use of pesticides.

Jane Goodall—Her study of chimpanzees in Africa gave the world a close-up look at how a population of animals lives.

Bruce Babbitt—As governor of Arizona and later as Secretary of the Interior, he has been a champion of the environment.

Food Webs

Question:
What would be the effect of removing an organism from the food web?

Materials:
set of Role Cards
large sheet of paper
ruler
pencil

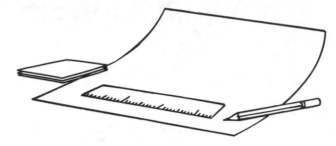

Prediction:
On your record sheet, predict which of the following organisms will be the most important in the food web: crab, phytoplankton, sperm whale, anchovy, flying fish, killer whale, dolphin, shark, zooplankton, squid, tuna, seabird, salmon, blue whale, or hatchetfish.

Procedure:
1. After you finish the outside activity, draw a circle on your large sheet of paper. Write the names of the organisms around the edges of the circle.
2. Draw arrows connecting each organism to the animal that eats it. Use your *Food Roles* sheet to decide which role each of the organisms plays.

Results:
What role does each of the organisms play? Write your results on your record sheet.

Conclusions:
Answer the following questions on your record sheet:

What would be the result of an oil spill that kills all the plankton?

Anchovies, such as the one in your food web, like warm water. If the climate changed and the water temperature became too cold, causing the anchovies to move to a new place in the ocean, what effect would this have on local tuna fishermen?

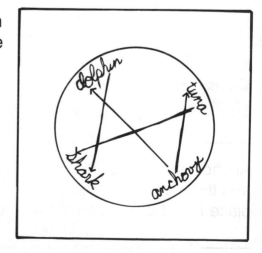

Food Webs

Question:
What would be the effect of removing an organism from the food web?
Prediction:
Which organism will be the most important in the food web?_____
Results:
What role does each of the organisms play?

Animal	Role
crab	_____
phytoplankton	_____
sperm whale	consumer, predator
anchovy	_____
flying fish	_____
killer whale	_____
dolphin	_____
shark	_____
zooplankton	_____
squid	_____
tuna	_____
seabird	_____
salmon	_____
blue whale	_____
hatchetfish	_____

Conclusions:
What would be the result of an oil spill that kills all the plankton?_____
_____

Anchovies, such as the one in your food web, like warm water. If the climate changed and the water temperature became too cold, causing the anchovies to move to a new place in the ocean, what effect would this have on local tuna fishermen?

_____

© FS-23214 Science Made Simple ▪ © Frank Schaffer Publications, Inc.

Food Roles

Producer: I make my own food using materials from the environment and sunlight.
I am a green plant or plantlike organism.

Consumer: I cannot make my own food and need to eat plants or other animals.

Predator: I catch and eat other living animals.

Prey: I am caught and eaten by other animals.

Decomposer: I eat the remains and wastes of animals and plants.

Name _____

Tuna

Diet: I eat anchovies.

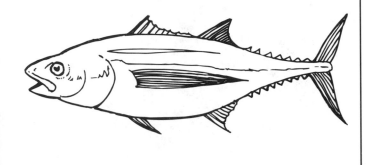

Seabird

Diet: I eat anchovies, flying fish, salmon, and zooplankton.

Sperm Whale

Diet: I eat squid and hatchetfish.

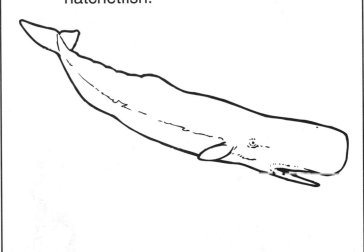

Blue Whale

Diet: I eat zooplankton.

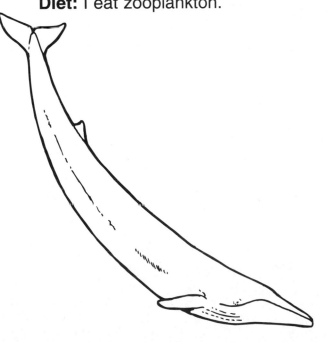

Dolphin

Diet: I eat squid, flying fish, and anchovies.

Flying Fish

Diet: I eat zooplankton.

Shark

Diet: I eat dolphin and tuna.

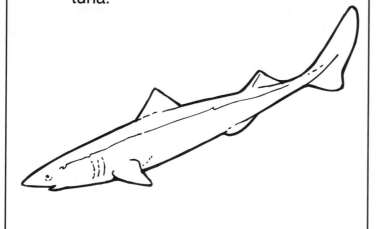

Phytoplankton

Diet: I make my own food by photosynthesis.

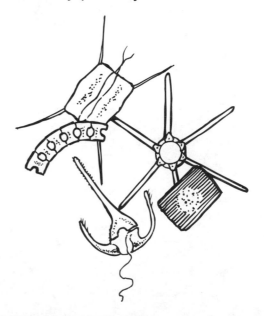

FS-23214 Science Made Simple ▪ © Frank Schaffer Publications, Inc.

Killer Whale

Diet: I eat dolphin, blue whale, and tuna.

Salmon

Diet: I eat anchovies and squid.

Anchovy

Diet: I eat zooplankton.

Squid

Diet: I eat anchovies and hatchetfish.

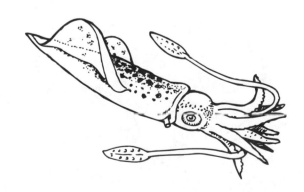

Zooplankton

Diet: I eat phytoplankton.

Crab

Diet: I eat all dead animals and plants.

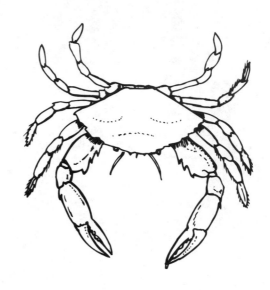

Hatchetfish

Diet: I eat zooplankton.

Food Pyramids

Food chains are often shown as food pyramids to demonstrate how energy is reduced as it passes through the food chain. Each level of the food chain does not pass along all the energy to the next level. Only about 10 percent of the energy contained in a prey's food is passed on to the predator. As your class organizes information from its food web into a pyramid, students will see that the total amount of animals of each species is related to its position on the pyramid. The largest animals are less numerous and on the top; the smallest animals are more numerous and on the bottom.

FOOD PYRAMIDS

Class Activity

Materials: copies of pages 18–19, set of Role Cards (pages 13–16)

Exploration: Students will be using the Role Cards and food web constructed from the previous activity. Explain to your class that besides predator, prey, consumer, and producer, animals are also put into categories according to where they are on the food chain. Animals that eat green plants are called *first-level consumers*. Animals that eat first-level consumers are called *second-level consumers*. Second-level consumers serve as food for *third-level consumers*. Third-level consumers serve as food for *fourth-level consumers*.

Give each student pages 18 and 19. Tell the students to find the animal from the Role Card set that eats green plants or plantlike organisms (such as phytoplankton) and write its name in the first-level consumers part of the pyramid. Have students choose a second-level consumer that would be a predator to the first-level consumer they chose and write its name on the pyramid. Third- and fourth-level consumers should be the predators of the animals below them.

Discovery: The total number of fourth-level consumers is small compared to the number of first-level consumers. For example, the single shark at the top of the food chain is compared to the millions of zooplankton at the bottom of the food chain. However, the size of the individual fourth-level consumer is much larger than the first-level consumer. The shark is much bigger than the microscopic zooplankton. The first-level consumer must have a large population and reproduce quickly and in great numbers in order to serve as food for the large upper-level animals. One exception is the baleen whale; on the food pyramid, it is located directly above the plankton.

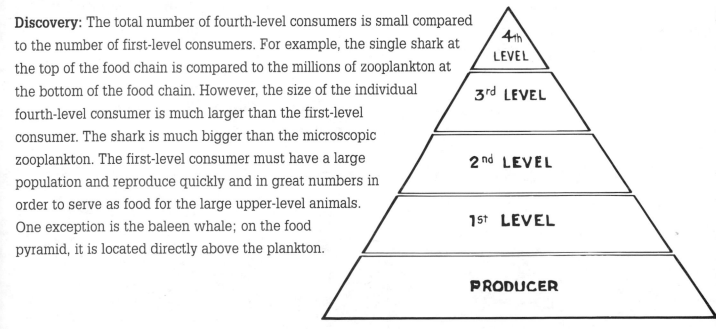

4th LEVEL

3rd LEVEL

2nd LEVEL

1st LEVEL

PRODUCER

Food Pyramids

Question:
How do the populations of the various organisms on the food pyramid compare with one another?

Prediction:
What would be the effect on the food pyramid if the second-level consumer's population increased in great numbers?

Materials:
set of Role Cards

Procedure and Results:
1. Using your role cards, find the producer and write its name at the bottom of the triangle.
2. Find an animal that eats the producer and write its name in the space label *First-level Consumer*.
3. Find an animal that eats the first-level consumer and write its name in the space above the first-level animal you wrote. Label the space *Second-level Consumer*.
4. If you can, find an animal that eats the second-level consumer. Add its name in the space above the second-level consumer. Label the space *Third-level Consumer*.
5. If you can, find an animal that eats the third-level consumer. Add its name in the space above the third-level consumer. Label the space *Fourth-level Consumer*.
6. Research the estimated world population for each animal or organism listed on your pyramid. Write the numbers in the corresponding spaces on the pyramid.

Conclusion:
Answer the following questions on your record sheet:
How do the various populations compare?

What did you notice about the size of the animal at the top of the food pyramid compared to the size of the animal at the bottom of the pyramid?

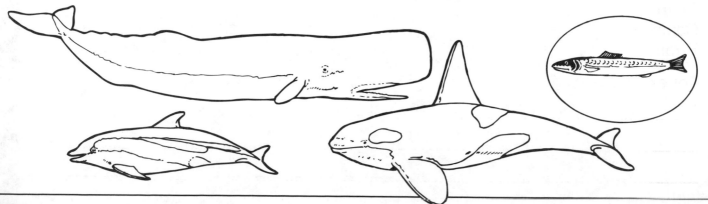

Food Pyramids

Question:
How do the populations of the various organisms on the food pyramid compare with one another?

Prediction:
What would be the effect on the food pyramid if the second-level consumer's population

increased in great numbers? _____

Results:

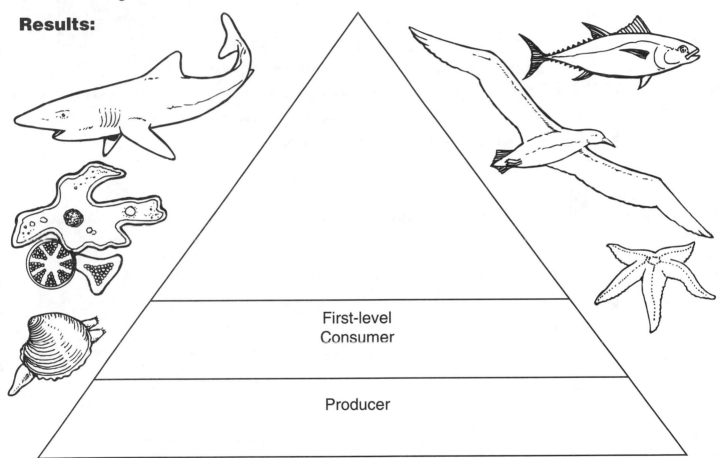

First-level
Consumer

Producer

Conclusion:
Compare the different populations. Also compare the size of the animal at the top of the pyramid with the size of the lower-level consumers and the producer below it.

For example, compare the sizes of a shark and the phytoplankton. _____

_____

_____

_____

Climates

Just as plants and animals interact in the environment, other factors affect living things. These are called the nonliving factors and include such things as water, air, soil, and temperature. For example, some living things can live and flourish in desert areas with very little water while others need an abundance of rain to survive. Ask your students what would happen to a cactus if you watered it too much. (*It would bloat and then die.*) What would happen to a tropical orchid that received only an inch or two of water per year? (*It would also die.*) Just as water influences the survival of living things, so does temperature. Various living things perform best at different temperatures. Temperature over a period of time is one of the important weather factors that make up the *climate* of a region. The climate of a very small area such as a lawn or grove of trees is called a *microclimate*.

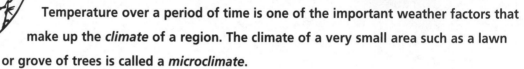

Art Project

Desert Dioramas

This activity will help your students discover facts about one particular climate—the desert.

Materials: shoebox, sand, white paper, crayons or markers, scissors, tagboard or light cardboard, tape

Give each student a shoebox or ask each child to bring one from home. Get books from the library about animals and plants that live in the desert. Let your students use the books to find out what is in a desert. Then have them put sand in the bottom of their shoeboxes to make dioramas. Ask the students to draw on paper some of the animals and plants that live in the desert. Have them color these drawings and glue them onto tagboard or any light cardboard. Let the students cut out the drawings and tape them in their dioramas.

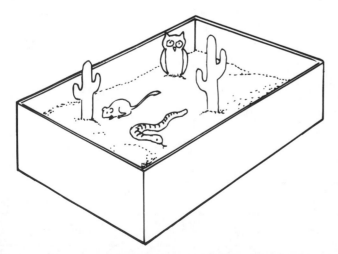

As a follow-up activity, have each student write a story about the animals and plants that live in his or her desert.

CLIMATES

Materials: copies of pages 22–23, yardstick, three thermometers with metal or paper backing, masking tape, pointed stick or sharpened pencil, ruler

Exploration: Ask your class to describe the temperature throughout the school day, starting with the time the students walked to school or waited for the school bus, through lunch and recess, and finally at dismissal. Write their descriptions on the blackboard. (*Examples: cool or foggy morning, breezy at lunchtime, and warm in the afternoon*)

Explain to your class that just as temperature changes throughout the day, it also varies from place to place at any given time. One part of the school may be cooler or warmer than the other. On the blackboard, write the areas of the school that may have different temperatures, both inside and outside. (*Children's responses should include air-conditioned rooms, the blacktop, under a tree, and in the sandbox.*) Draw a picture of a mountain on the blackboard. Ask your class which part of the mountain is the coolest? (*They should respond that the top is the coolest and that is why snow falls on the tops of mountains.*) Hold up a yardstick and ask the class which temperature should be the warmest, the temperature at the top of the stick or the temperature at the bottom? Next, tell your students that they are going to find out the different temperatures that exist between the top of the yardstick and the bottom.

Each group will tape a thermometer to the ends of its yardstick to create a "temperature stick." Tell your students that they will take measurements holding the temperature stick straight upright. Each location where they record temperature requires the stick to remain still for five minutes before recording. Ask the class why. (*It takes that long for the thermometer to change completely.*) The places where they will record temperatures are the classroom, the blacktop, in the shade, the sandbox, and the play field. They will see the differences in temperature in some places below ground, above ground, and at one yard/meter in height.

The first area they will explore is the classroom. Next, students will record temperatures on the blacktop in the sun. The third area will be a paved area that is in the shade of a tree. The fourth area will be the sandbox, where students will use the third thermometer to record the temperature below the surface using the ruler to measure five inches below ground. The final area to be studied will be an unpaved area in the sun, where students will again use the temperature stick and the third thermometer to record belowground temperatures. Students can use the pointed stick to make a five-inch-deep hole in which to place the thermometer.

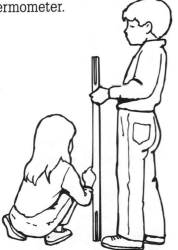

Discovery: In any given spot, the temperature will vary by altitude. Animals and plants will live in the area where they can survive best. The earthworm prefers the shade; the insects the sunlight. In areas of extreme heat, such as the desert, animals must hide in the shade until it gets dark or live underground for all or part of their life. Plants must also adapt to the nonliving part of the environment. Extreme changes in the climate, such as drought or flood, can drastically affect all living things in the ecosystem.

Climates

Thermometer ——

Tape ——

Question:
How does height affect temperature?

Prediction:
Which level—below ground, ground level, above ground—will have the highest temperatures? Write your prediction on your record sheet.

Materials:
one yardstick
three thermometers with metal or paper backing
masking tape
pointed stick or sharpened pencil
ruler

Procedure and Results:
1. Attach two of the thermometers to the yardstick using the tape as shown. Be careful not to break the thermometers. This is your temperature stick.
2. In your classroom, place the temperature stick upright on the floor. Wait five minutes and read the thermometers on the temperature stick on the top and bottom. Write the temperatures on your record sheet.
3. Go outside on the playground in the sunlight. Hold the stick upright with the bottom on the ground. Wait five minutes and read the thermometers on the top and bottom of the temperature stick. Write the temperatures on your record sheet.
4. Find a paved area in the shade and repeat the experiment, making sure to wait five minutes before reading the temperatures. Write the temperatures on the record sheet.
5. Go to the sandbox and repeat the experiment. This time, insert the third thermometer five inches below the surface using the ruler to measure. Read the three temperatures after five minutes and write the results on your record sheet.
6. Go to an area with soil that is not in the shade. Use your stick to make a five-inch hole. Insert the thermometer. Repeat the experiment and record your results on your record sheet.

Conclusions:
Answer the following questions on your record sheet:

Were the temperatures higher at the top of the temperature stick or at the bottom?

Why do you think that happened?

FS-23214 Science Made Simple ▪ © Frank Schaffer Publications, Inc.

Name _____

Climates

Question:
How does height affect temperature?

Prediction:
Which level—below ground, ground level, above ground—will have the highest temperatures?

_____

_____

Results:
Record the temperatures in the chart below.

Place	Temperature at Top	Temperature at Bottom	Underground Temperature
Classroom			
Playground			
Shade			
Sandbox			
Soil			

Conclusions:
Were the temperatures higher at the top of the temperature stick or at the bottom?

_____

Why do you think that happened?_____

_____

_____

Decomposers

Decomposers are an important part of the food chain. They break down the individual cells and allow materials to be released into the environment, where they can be reused. An example of a decomposer is *fungi*. As you give your class opportunities to explore the effects of decomposers, your students will begin to see what the world would look like if decomposers did not do their job.

DECOMPOSERS

Group Experiment

Materials: package of yeast, warm water, microscope, mushrooms or picture of mushrooms, copies of pages 25–26, two slices of fresh fruit (banana or peach—not apple), two zip-lock bags, one teaspoon dry yeast, masking tape, marker

Exploration: Bring some mushrooms to school or get a picture of mushrooms to show your class. Explain that mushrooms are an example of a *fungus*, a form of life that is neither animal nor plant. Fungi get their food from dead plant and animal material. **Remind children not to pick up mushrooms growing wild because many of them are deadly.**

Open the yeast package and add warm water to the yeast according to package directions. Using a microscope, allow the children to observe the yeast. Explain that yeast are fungi.

Give each group its materials. Tell the students to put a slice of fruit in one bag and seal the bag. Tell them to dip the same kind of fruit in one teaspoon of the dry yeast and then place it in the other bag. Place the bags in a dark place and have students check them daily for one week and record their observations. **Caution your students not to eat the fruit or open the bags at any time during the experiment. As molds grow, they may produce toxins or poisons. Some illnesses have been blamed on contact with molds. It is best to avoid contact with molds and to avoid inhaling their spores.**

Discovery: Fungi, which include the common bread mold as well as mushrooms, serve an important role in the ecosystem. Since they lack the ability to make their own food, they are either harmful parasites getting their food from other living things or they are *saprophytes*, organisms that break down already dead organisms.

NATURE WALK

Class Activity

Explore a wooded area near your school with your class. Find an old fallen tree or an old tree stump. If you live in a urban area, look for an old rotted tree trunk to examine in the area near your school. Have students examine the animals that live near the tree. These animals also serve to break down the tree.

Decomposers

Question:
What effect will yeast have on the decomposition of fruit?

Prediction:
How many days will pass before fruit starts to decompose?
Write your prediction on your record sheet.

Materials:
two slices of fresh fruit (banana or peach—not apple)
two zip-lock bags
one teaspoon dry yeast
masking tape
marker

Procedure:
1. Place one slice of fruit into a plastic bag and seal the bag. Put your name on the bag with the tape.
2. Dip the other slice of fruit in the yeast so that both sides are covered. Place the fruit in the other bag and seal it. Put the word *Yeast* and your name on the bag with the tape.
3. Place both bags in an area that will be dark and warm.
4. Observe the bags every day for one week. Do not open or touch the contents of the bags. **Caution: Allergic reactions due to mold are very common. As molds grow, they produce toxins or poisons. Some illnesses have been blamed on contact with molds. It is wise to avoid contact with molds and to avoid inhaling their spores.**

Results:
Describe the contents of each bag daily on your record sheet.

Conclusion:
Use your results to support the following statement on your record sheet: "Without fungi, the world would become crowded with dead matter."

Decomposers

Question:
What effect will yeast have on the decomposition of fruit?

Prediction:
How many days will pass before fruit starts to decompose?_____

_____

Results:
Describe the contents of each bag daily.

	Fruit Without Yeast	Fruit With Yeast
Day 1		
Day 2		
Day 3		
Day 4		
Day 5		

Conclusion:
Use your results to support this statement:
"Without fungi, the world would become crowded with dead matter."_____

_____

_____

FS-23214 Science Made Simple ▪ © Frank Schaffer Publications, Inc.

Landfills

While decomposers may work in the food chain, human populations cannot leave their wastes around to decompose without causing health hazards or attracting insects and other vermin. Disposing of solid wastes is a major problem for human civilizations. As you give your students opportunities to examine their own habits regarding solid wastes, they will begin to come up with solutions for reducing the amount of solid wastes their families produce each day.

FAMILY TRASH

Class Activity

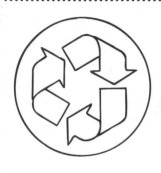

Have students list the items in their families' trash daily for a week. Do not have them include food items, only the food containers. Ask them to check the bottom of each plastic item to see if it has a recyclable symbol. If so, have them mark it on the list with an *R*. Each day, sort the list into one of five headings: *Paper, Plastic, Metal, Glass,* or *Other*. At the end of the week, make bar graphs of each type of trash. Have students decide which trash type they could reduce; which type they could reuse for other purposes; and which they could recycle.

LANDFILLS

Group Experiment

Materials: copies of pages 28–29, two 4-inch squares of newspaper, two small pieces of plastic foam, two aluminum nails, two pieces of fruit, small paper bag, small zip-lock bag, trowel

Exploration: After your students have examined their families' trash habits, remind them that there are several ways we dispose of our solid wastes. Ask students how the trash can be disposed and write their answers on the blackboard. (*Dumping in the ocean, burning, burying in landfills, or recycling are possibilities.*) For each answer, ask the students to propose a problem associated with the suggestion. (*Examples: Dumps cause diseases and attract rats and other vermin; ocean dumping kills marine life; burning causes air pollution; landfills take up a lot of space.*) Find out from your local trash collector how trash is handled in your area. Most communities now bury their trash in sanitary landfills. Explain to your students that they are going to construct a small model of what occurs every day in landfills across the country.

Give each group its materials. Each group will fill both a paper bag and a zip-lock bag with the same trash materials. Using a small trowel, the students will bury their bags for one month. At the end of the month, they will examine the contents of the bags.

Discovery: In each bag, only the food items will show decomposition. The other items will show little effect of breaking down. Regardless of paper or plastic bags, landfills do not offer a solution to trash reduction.

Landfills

Question:
What is the difference, if any, between using paper or plastic garbage bags?

Prediction:
Do you think trash will decompose better in a paper bag or in a plastic bag, or do you think it doesn't make a difference? Write your prediction on your record sheet.

Materials:
two 4-inch squares of newspaper
two small pieces of plastic foam
two aluminum nails
two pieces of fruit
small paper bag
small zip-lock plastic bag
trowel

Procedure:
1. Place a piece of newspaper, plastic foam, fruit, and a nail into the paper bag.
2. Repeat step one using a zip-lock bag. Put your names on each bag.
3. In an area that will not be disturbed, dig a hole and bury the bags so that they are completely covered and will be undisturbed for one month.
4. At the end of one month, dig up the bags and carefully examine the contents.

Results:
Describe the contents of each bag. Write your observations on your record sheet.

Conclusion:
Answer the following questions on your record sheet:
Which type of bag would you recommend to be put in a landfill? Why?

FS-23214 Science Made Simple ▪ © Frank Schaffer Publications, Inc.

Name _____

 **L**andfills

Question:

What is the difference, if any, between using paper or plastic garbage bags?

Prediction:

Do you think trash will decompose better in a paper bag or in a plastic bag, or do you

think it doesn't make a difference? _____

Results:

After burying the bags for one month, describe the contents of each bag.

	Plastic Bag	**Paper Bag**
newspaper		
plastic foam		
fruit		
nail		

Conclusion:

Which type of bag would you recommend to be put in a landfill? Why? _____

_____

_____

_____

Physical Science

Children see change occurring all around them. A bicycle left in the rain gets rusty. They see their parents mixing ingredients in the kitchen and producing cookies or bread. Bubbles appear mysteriously when tablets are added to water. As they get older, children start to notice the position and motion of objects. As they continue to try and make sense of the forces and motion occurring around them, they ask the much bigger question, "What changes and forces will affect my life, today and in the future?"

CONCEPTS

The ideas and activities in this section will help children explore the following concepts:

• Mixtures are made of substances that are not chemically changed and can be physically separated.

• Chemical changes result in new substances that cannot be separated into the original components.

• Force is the name given to pushes and pulls.

• Gravity is the name given to the force that Earth exerts on other objects.

• An object can be acted on by multiple forces.

LITERATURE RESOURCES

These books are recommended as resources to help students learn about physical science.

The Way Things Work by David Macaulay (Houghton Mifflin, 1988). From levers to lasers, cars to computers, the author provides a visual guide to the world of machines.

Invention Book by Steven Caney (Workman, 1985). Everything you need to know about inventions, including at-home projects, are in this book for the young inventor. Thirty-six stories of great American inventions are included.

Inventions by Lionel Bender (Knopf, 1991). Inventions throughout time are presented in this well-illustrated book in the Eyewitness Books series.

FS-23214 Science Made Simple ▪ © Frank Schaffer Publications, Inc.

Reactions and Interactions

Mixtures are made of two or more substances that are not chemically changed. Since no new linkages are formed, nor are linkages broken, the existing linkages are only intermingled and can be physically separated by methods such as distillation, filtration, and chromatography. Chemical changes result in new substances that cannot be separated into the original components. Some chemical reactions occur spontaneously without any energy needed. Other chemical reactions may need energy such as heat to start the reaction.

WHAT COLOR IS BLACK?

Group Experiment

Materials: copies of pages 32–33, black water-based marker, water-based markers in various colors, white paper towel or basket-type coffee filter, scissors, pencil, glass jar about six inches high, water, ruler, cellophane tape, food coloring, toothpicks

Exploration: Give each group a white paper towel or one basket-type coffee filter and ask them to cut it into 2" x 8" strips. Tell your students that they will be finding what color of inks are in their black markers. Each group will measure two inches from the long end of one of the strips and make a small dot using their black water-based marker. Taping this strip to a pencil, they will place the pencil over a jar of water and slowly lower the strip into the water, making sure only the very end of the paper-towel strip touches the water. As water climbs slowly up the strip, the colors of the ink will be seen separating. Students will repeat this procedure using other colors of water-based marking pens and food coloring. Toothpicks should be used to transfer the food coloring. **Caution: Care should be taken since clothes may be stained permanently by the food coloring.**

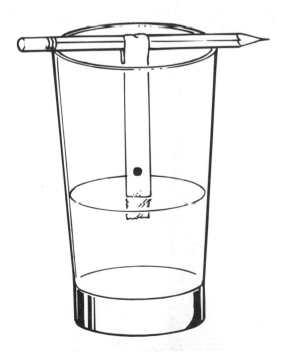

Discovery: The colors within the markers and food coloring are mixtures and can be physically separated using the process of chromatography. As water rises up the paper-towel strips by capillary action, the different dyes are carried along at different rates, depending on the solubility of each component and how much each component adheres to the paper. The most soluble component will move farthest up. The less soluble or more strongly absorbed components will move a shorter distance. Thus the components physically separate. If two components travel the same rate and distance, they are the same. If one blue spot travels two inches and the other travels five inches, then they are different substances.

What Color Is Black?

Question:
What colored dyes make up the color of a black marker?

Prediction:
On your record sheet, predict what colored dyes make up the color in black markers.

Materials:
black water-based marker
water-based markers in different colors
white paper towel or coffee filter
scissors
ruler

pencils
glass jar about six inches high
water
cellophane tape
toothpicks

Procedure:
1. Cut the paper towel or coffee filter into 2" x 8" strips.
2. Use a pencil to mark a line two inches from the end of each strip.
3. Make a small dot with the black marker on the line of one strip.
4. Tape the other end of the strip onto the pencil and roll the strip around the pencil.
5. Pour one inch of water into the jar.
6. Slowly lower the strip into the water so that just the edge of the strip is touching the water and the dot is above the water. (Do not let the strip touch the sides of the jar.)
7. Observe over 10 minutes as water climbs the strip.
8. Let the strip dry.
9. Repeat the steps above using different colored markers or food coloring. If using food coloring, use toothpicks to make the small dots.

Results:
Record the colors you see in the chart on your record sheet and compare the results to your predictions.

Conclusion:
Answer the following question on your record sheet.
Why is this experiment an example of a physical change?

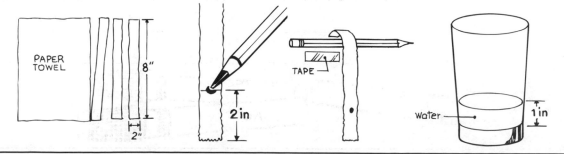

FS-23214 Science Made Simple ■ © Frank Schaffer Publications, Inc.

What Color Is Black?

Question:
What colored dyes make up the color of a black marker?

Prediction:
What colored dyes make up the colors in markers? List the original colors and write your predictions in the chart below.

Results:
After doing the experiment, record the results in the chart.

Original Color	Prediction	Results
black		

Conclusion:
Why is this experiment an example of physical change? (Use your results to help you

answer.) _____

_____

_____

_____

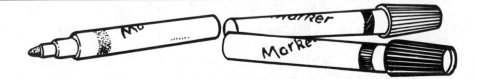

RUST

Materials: copies of pages 35–36, two large test tubes, two small wads of steel wool, flat pan, one-fourth cup of vinegar in a cup, ruler, clock, water

Exploration: Ask your students to give examples of things around their homes that rust. Write their responses on the blackboard. (*Possible answers include fences, bicycles, nails, and cars.*) If there is time, you may want to conduct a quick tour around the school and look for evidence of rust. Explain to the class that rust is a product of a chemical change. In order for rust to form, certain conditions must be met. Ask the students what these conditions might be. (*Water and iron are the answers most children may guess. Oxygen is the other correct answer that they will discover in the activity.*)

Each group will soak one steel wool wad in vinegar for one minute and gently squeeze the vinegar out. The students will place the wads into a test tube. The other dry wad of steel wool will also be placed in a test tube. Students will place the test tubes upside down and make sure the wads will not fall out. Then the groups will stand the test tubes open-end down in the pan with water. Observing the test tubes carefully at five-minute intervals for 30 minutes, the students will observe and measure if water has entered either tube. Caution groups not to disturb the tubes. At the end of 35 minutes, they will examine the steel wool wads.

Discovery: During oxidation, oxygen and iron combined and formed iron oxide, or rust. As oxygen was used, water rose up the tube to replace the oxygen. The untreated steel wool has a grease covering to reduce oxidation. The vinegar removed the grease.

THAT'S A GAS!

Caution: This activity involves the use of a lighted match. Safety rules should be reviewed.

Materials: copies of pages 37–38, funnel, eight-ounce glass, four ounces of water, test tube, two seltzer tablets, match

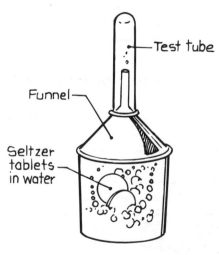

Test tube

Funnel

Seltzer tablets in water

Exploration: Tell your class that some chemical reactions take place without any energy needed. These reactions are called *spontaneous reactions*. The following activity will show such a reaction. Each group will put water into a glass. After inverting a funnel so that it points upward and covering the end of the funnel with a test tube that is turned upside down, they will add seltzer tablets to the water and quickly cover the glass with the funnel/test tube apparatus. They need to be sure to collect all gas into the test tube and not let any escape from the sides of the funnel. Being very careful not to turn the test tube over and keeping it upside down, they will place a lighted match into the test tube and watch what happens. (You may wish to add the match yourself.)

Discovery: The gas bubbles that are produced are carbon dioxide. The burning match will be extinguished. Some fire extinguishers work by producing carbon dioxide and cutting off oxygen from the fire.

Rust

Question:
What conditions are necessary for rust to form?

Prediction:
In which test tube will rust form—one containing steel wool soaked in vinegar or one with untreated steel wool? Write your prediction on your record sheet.

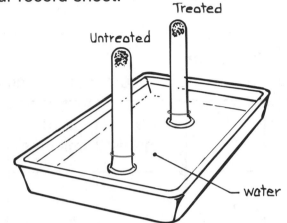

Materials:
two large test tubes
two wads of steel wool
flat pan
water
one-fourth cup of vinegar in a cup
ruler
clock

Procedure:
1. Place one wad of steel wool in a test tube and push it down to the end so that it will not fall.
2. Soak the other wad of steel wool in one-fourth cup of vinegar.
3. Gently squeeze the vinegar out of the steel wool and place it in the other test tube, pushing it down to the end so it will not fall.
4. Place one-half inch of water in the pan and place the test tubes upside down in the water.
5. Observe at five-minute intervals to see if water has entered either tube and measure its height if it has. Record your measurements. Do not knock over the tubes or disturb them. It usually takes at least 25 minutes to see the difference in the tubes.
6. At the end of 35 minutes, measure the final amount of water. Remove both wads and describe their appearance.

Results:
Write your observations on your record sheet.

Conclusions:
Answer the following questions on your record sheet:

Chemical change involves new compounds being formed. What new substance was formed?

Explain what happened in the two tubes and why.

Rust

Question:
What conditions are necessary for rust to form?

Prediction:
In which test tube will rust form—one containing steel wool soaked in vinegar or one with untreated steel wool?

_____

Results:
Record the measurements of the amount of water at five-minute intervals.

	5 minutes	10 minutes	15 minutes	20 minutes	25 minutes	30 minutes	35 minutes
test tube #1							
test tube #2							

What is the appearance of the vinegar-soaked wad?_____

_____

What is the appearance of the untreated wad?_____

_____

Conclusions:
Chemical change involves new compounds being formed. What new substance was

formed in this activity?_____

_____

Explain what happened in the two tubes and why._____

THaT's a Gas!

Question:
What gas is produced when a seltzer tablet is added to water?

Prediction:
What will happen to the flame of a match when you expose it to the gas produced from a seltzer-tablet-and-water reaction? Write your prediction on your record sheet.

Materials:

funnel	test tube
eight-ounce glass	two seltzer tablets
four ounces of water	match

Caution: This experiment involves the use of an open flame. Follow all safety rules.

Procedure:
1. Put four ounces of water into the glass. Turn over the funnel so that the pointed end is facing up and cover the opening with the test tube with the opening pointed down.
2. Make sure that the funnel will completely cover the opening of the glass. If not, use paper and tape to make sure the top will be covered. Add the seltzer tablets to the water and quickly cover with the funnel/test tube combination. Do not turn the test tube back over.
3. When the seltzer tablet reaction is finished, remove the test tube still holding it upside down. Carefully insert a lighted match up into the test tube. **Use care when dealing with fire.**

Results:
Observe and describe what happened when you added the seltzer tablets. Observe and describe what happened when you put the lighted match into the test tube. Write your observations on your record sheet.

Conclusion:
Answer the following questions on your record sheet:

Is this experiment an example of a chemical change or a physical change? Explain your answer.

What gas do you think was in the tube? Explain your guess.

That's a Gas!

Question:
What gas is produced when a seltzer tablet is added to water?

Prediction:
What will happen to the flame of a match when you expose it to

the gas produced from a seltzer-tablet-and-water reaction?

_____

_____

_____

Results:
Observe and describe what happened in the experiment.

What happened when you added the seltzer tablet to the water?_____

_____

What happened when you put the lighted match into the test tube?_____

_____

Conclusions:
Is this experiment an example of a chemical change or a physical change? Explain your

answer._____

_____

_____

_____

What gas do you think was in the tube? Explain your guess._____

_____

_____

_____

_____

FS-23214 Science Made Simple ■ © Frank Schaffer Publications, Inc.

WHICH DOUGH WILL GROW?

Ask your students to raise their hands if they have ever seen bread being made. Ask the class to think about the steps of breadmaking. Elicit responses and write them on the blackboard. (*Possible answers include mixing the ingredients, kneading the dough, and baking the bread.*) Tell the class that breadmaking involves a chemical reaction that occurs between the yeast, which is a form of fungi, and sugar. The chemical reaction is called *fermentation*. The yeast will "eat" the sugar and release carbon dioxide gas. This gas will cause the dough to rise. Yeast is also used to make beer and wine.

Materials: copies of pages 40–41, four egg-sized balls of yeast dough, four small paper plates, jar of hot water, ruler, lamp with 100-watt bulb, ice chest with ice in it, four thermometers

Preparation: Dough can be prepared in advance from any yeast-based recipe or, for simplicity, purchased from the frozen food section. Dough is available as loaves or may be purchased already divided as rolls. Allow the dough to defrost in a room that is not too warm or in the refrigerator overnight.

Exploration: Your students will predict which temperatures (hot, warm, room temperature, or cold) will cause the bread to rise higher. They will place their samples in the various locations and observe and measure the dough every half-hour for three hours. A thermometer will be placed in each location to record the temperature. Hot water needs to be replaced every 30 minutes. Remind students not to disturb the dough by poking it. Caution everyone not to eat the dough.

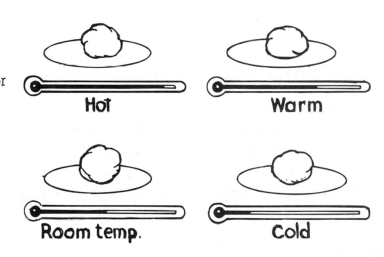

Hot   Warm

Room temp.   Cold

Discovery: Yeast grows best at 80°–90° F. (25°–30° C.). Temperatures that are too high will kill the yeast and temperatures that are too low will cause the yeast to "rest," or be inactive. The carbon dioxide that the yeast releases is an example of a chemical reaction that occurs in living things.

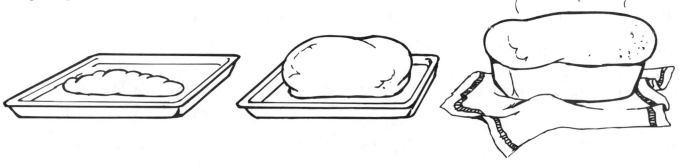

Which Dough Will Grow?

Question:
How does temperature affect a chemical reaction?

Prediction:
What temperature will cause the bread to rise
the greatest in three hours? Write your
prediction on your record sheet.

Materials:
four egg-sized balls of yeast dough
four small paper plates
jar of hot water
ruler
lamp with 100-watt bulb
ice chest with ice in it
four thermometers

Caution: Do not taste anything used in this experiment.

Procedure:
1. Place each ball of dough on a paper plate and mark your name(s) on each plate.
2. Put one plate under the 100-watt bulb lamp, one in the ice chest, and one over the jar that is filled with hot water. Leave one plate at room temperature.
3. Observe your samples every 30 minutes. Replace the hot water in the jar with new hot water every 30 minutes. Do not poke the ball of dough.

Results:
Observe the dough every 30 minutes. Measure the height each time you observe the dough. Write your observations and measurements on your record sheet.

Conclusions:
Answer the following questions on your record sheet:

How does temperature affect bread rising? Use your data in your answer.

Why do people wait three
hours before putting
bread dough in the oven?

100-watt
bulb

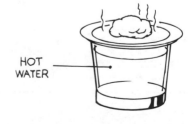

HOT
WATER

FS-23214 *Science Made Simple* ▪ © Frank Schaffer Publications, Inc.

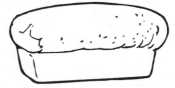

Which Dough Will Grow?

Question:
How does temperature affect a chemical reaction?

Prediction:
What temperature will cause bread dough to rise the most in three hours?

_____

_____

Results:
Observe the dough every 30 minutes. Measure the height each time you observe the dough. Write your observations below.

location	30 minutes	60 minutes	90 minutes	120 minutes	150 minutes	180 minutes
lamp						
hot water						
room temperature						
ice chest						

Conclusions:
How does temperature affect bread rising? Use your data to help you. _____

_____

_____

Why do people wait three hours before putting bread dough in the oven? _____

_____

_____

_____

THE GAS WE BREATHE

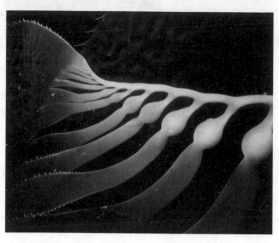

Ask your class if anyone knows what photosynthesis is. *Photosynthesis* is the life process by which green plants use sunlight, chlorophyll, carbon dioxide, and water to make oxygen and food in the form of sugar. The food that the green plants produce provides nourishment for the animals above it in the food chain. Plants, like animals, also "breathe," but they take in carbon dioxide and release oxygen.

Materials: copies of pages 43–44, elodea (a common water plant sold in fish stores), clear funnel, test tube that will fit over the tip of the funnel, water, bright light, wooden splint, match

Caution: This experiment involves an open flame. Review safety rules.

Exploration: Tell your students to fill the large bowl or beaker with water. The elodea will be placed inside and covered with the large end of the funnel. The tip of the funnel must be under water. The test tube will be filled with water and covered with a thumb so that no water escapes. The test tube will be inverted and, with no air entering, placed over the funnel. After several hours under bright light, the test tube will contain little, if any, water. Lifting the still-inverted test tube, they should allow any water that may remain to drain. (The test tube must remain inverted.) Then a child will carefully light a wooden splint and blow out the flame, leaving only the glowing splint. The child will quickly place the glowing splint inside the inverted test tube. (You may wish to light the match and place the glowing splint inside the test tube yourself.)

Discovery: Photosynthesis produced the gas oxygen. The pressure of the oxygen pushed the water out of the tube and into the bowl. The glowing splint burst into flame. Plants in the ocean produce oxygen for the animals in the ocean as well as provide food.

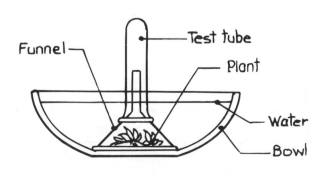

The Gas We Breathe

Question:
What is the name of the gas produced by elodea?

Prediction:
What will happen when a glowing splint is placed in the gas produced by an elodea plant? Write your prediction on the record sheet.

Materials:
elodea
clear funnel
test tube that will fit over the tip of the funnel
water
bright light
wooden splint
match

Procedure:
1. Fill the large bowl with water. Place the elodea inside.
2. Cover the elodea with the large end of the funnel, so that the tip of the funnel is still under water.
3. Fill the test tube with water. Using your thumb to make sure no water runs out, invert the test tube and put it over the small end of the funnel. No air can enter the test tube.
4. Put the experiment in a bright light for at least three hours. Observe every 30 minutes.
5. Carefully lift the test tube, still inverted. Allow any water still in the tube to drain. Keep the test tube upside down.
6. Light a wooden splint and blow it out gently, leaving a glowing end.
   Quickly place the glowing splint into the inverted test tube.

Results:
Record your observations every 30 minutes on your record sheet.

Conclusions:
Answer the following questions on your record sheet:

What happened to the glowing splint? Why?

How does this apply to plants and animals in the ocean?

The Gas We Breathe

Question:
What is the name of the gas produced by elodea?

Prediction:
What will happen when a glowing splint is placed in the gas produced by an elodea plant?

Results:
Record your observations below every 30 minutes.

Time	Observations
30 minutes	
60 minutes	
90 minutes	
120 minutes	
150 minutes	
180 minutes	

Conclusions:
What happened to the glowing splint? Why?_____

_____

How does this apply to plants and animals in the ocean?_____

_____

Forces and Motion

A *force* is any push or pull on an object that causes that object to move or causes a moving object to slow, stop, or change direction. Examples of forces include gravity and friction. *Gravity* is the name given to the force that the Earth exerts on other objects. *Friction* is a force that slows down moving objects. *Simple machines* are tools that change the force applied to them to do work more easily. We define *work* as moving an object by using a force. Moving objects that are thrown, shot, hit, or hurled forward are called *projectiles*. Projectiles are influenced by forces.

THE AMAZING FALLING CUP
Group Activity

Materials: copies of pages 46–47, two plastic foam cups, water, chair, pencil

Exploration: Since this activity can be messy, it is suggested that it be done outside. Students need to be cautioned that they may get wet. Read with the class the directions on page 46. A small hole will be poked in the center of each cup. One cup will be filled with water and the students will observe that water will come out of the hole. The cup will be filled again, this time with the hole covered with a finger so that the water cannot escape. Someone will get on the chair and hold the cup by the rim letting the water escape slowly. The cup will be released so that it falls straight and everyone will observe what happens to the water coming out of the hole. Repeat the activity to be sure students see what happened. Students will record their results on page 47. (This activity is more dramatic if cups are dropped from greater heights such as a second-floor window or a ladder.)

Discovery: The first time, gravity pulled on the water, causing it to come out of the hole. When the cup was released, gravity pulled equally on the cup and the water and they fell at the same rate. Therefore, it appeared that water was not coming out of the hole. It appears that gravity has disappeared. This condition is called *microgravity*. It is the reason that astronauts appear to be floating in space. In reality, both the astronauts and the spacecraft are falling in space.

BIOGRAPHIES
Class Activity

Have students research the following famous scientists:

Sir Isaac Newton—This famous scientist researched gravity and motion and invented the reflecting telescope.

Galileo Galilei—For his discoveries, this scientist was threatened with death and condemned to house arrest.

Marie Curie—Her discoveries resulted in her becoming the first female recipient of a Nobel Prize.

Robert Goddard—His work with rockets laid the foundation for modern space travel.

The Amazing Falling Cup

Question:
What are the effects of gravity when dropping a leaking cup?

Prediction:
What will happen to the water when you drop a leaking cup from a height? Write your prediction on your record sheet.

Materials:
two plastic foam cups
water
chair
pencil

Procedure:
1. Using a pencil, poke a small hole in the bottom of each cup.
2. Fill one cup with water and observe what happens.
3. Fill the cup with water again, this time covering the hole with a finger so that the water cannot escape.
4. Climb onto a chair and hold the cup by the rim. Remove your finger from the hole and let the water escape slowly. Release the cup allowing it to fall straight down. Observe what happens to the water coming out of the hole.
5. Repeat step four with the other cup.

Results:
Observe what happened when the cup was held. Observe what happened when the cup was dropped. Write your observations on your record sheet.

Conclusions:
Answer the following questions on your record sheet:

What force was acting on the water the first time?

What force was acting on the water and cup the second time?

Why do you think the water acted the way it did the second time?

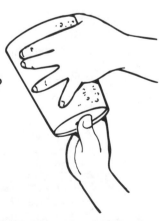

FS-23214 Science Made Simple ▪ © Frank Schaffer Publications, Inc.

Name _____

The Amazing Falling Cup

Question:
What are the effects of gravity when dropping a leaking cup?

Prediction:
What will happen to the water when you drop a leaking cup from a height?

_____

_____

Results:
Write your observations below.

What happened when you held the cup the first time? _____

_____

What happened when you dropped the cup? _____

_____

Conclusions:
What force was acting on the water the first time? _____

_____

What force was acting on the water and cup the second time? _____

_____

Why do you think the water acted the way it did the second time? _____

_____

_____

_____

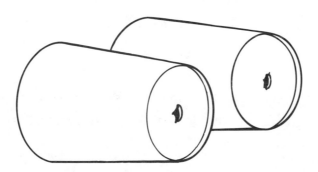

PENNY SLIDE

Materials: four thick books, ruler, penny, waxed paper, construction paper, cellophane, piece of carpet, piece of linoleum

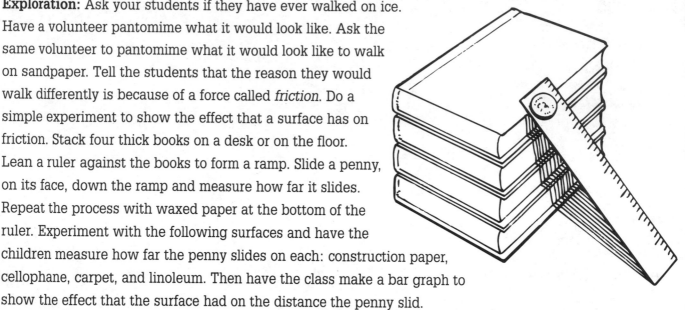

Exploration: Ask your students if they have ever walked on ice. Have a volunteer pantomime what it would look like. Ask the same volunteer to pantomime what it would look like to walk on sandpaper. Tell the students that the reason they would walk differently is because of a force called *friction*. Do a simple experiment to show the effect that a surface has on friction. Stack four thick books on a desk or on the floor. Lean a ruler against the books to form a ramp. Slide a penny, on its face, down the ramp and measure how far it slides. Repeat the process with waxed paper at the bottom of the ruler. Experiment with the following surfaces and have the children measure how far the penny slides on each: construction paper, cellophane, carpet, and linoleum. Then have the class make a bar graph to show the effect that the surface had on the distance the penny slid.

CENTER OF GRAVITY

Materials: copies of pages 49–51, 8 ½" x 11" sheet of cardboard, scissors, belt, paper plate, 10 inches of string, ruler, large paper clip, washer or heavy weight

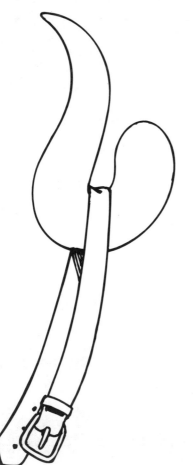

Exploration: Have each group cut out the *Center of Gravity Form* (page 50) and then trace it on a piece of thick cardboard. Cardboard from corrugated boxes works best. After cutting out the form, students will place the belt in the form as shown. By balancing the form, your class will discover the center of gravity.

Use the paper plate to find its center of gravity. Finding the center of gravity on the whole plate will be easy. The plate will then be cut in half using a curved line. Four holes will be punched around the shape and weighted string will be hung from three of the holes using a bent paper clip. The string's path will be traced from each hole to where the string crosses the shape's edge. Where the three lines intersect will determine the center of gravity.

Discovery: The center of gravity is the point at which an object balances. Tightrope walkers use a pole to lower their center of gravity, which makes them more stable than walking alone or stretching out their arms for balance.

Center of Gravity

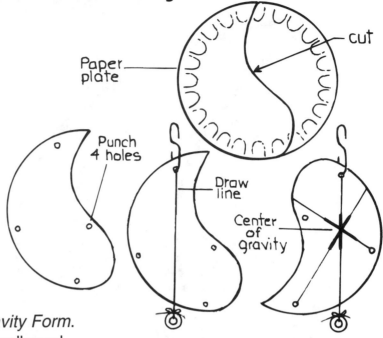

Question:
What is the center of gravity?

Materials:
8½" x 11" piece of cardboard
scissors
belt
paper plate
10 inches of string
heavy washer or weight
ruler
large paper clip

Procedure:
1. Carefully cut out the *Center of Gravity Form.*
   Trace the form onto the piece of cardboard.
   Cut out the cardboard, being sure to follow the lines exactly.
2. Place a belt into the form and balance the form upon your finger, upon a book, and upon a shelf.
3. Try to find the center of gravity of the paper plate by balancing it on your finger.
4. Cut the paper plate in half using a curved line as shown. Make four holes around the edge of the shape.
5. Attach a washer to the string and attach the string to a bent large paper clip.
6. Suspend the form by inserting the paper clip into one of the holes. Mark where the string crosses the form's edge. Use a ruler to draw a line from that mark to the hole you suspended the form from. The center of gravity must have been below the clip and on that line.
7. Repeat using two different holes. Where the three lines cross is the center of gravity. Try balancing from this point using your finger.

Conclusions:
Answer the following questions on your record sheet:

Is the center of gravity always in the center of an object? Use your observations to explain.

Try finding the center of gravity of your pencil. Explain why it is at the location you find it.

Center of Gravity Form

Center of Gravity

Question:
What is the center of gravity?

Conclusions:
Is the center of gravity always in the center of an object? Use your observations to

explain. _____

_____

_____

_____

Try finding the center of gravity of your pencil. Explain why it is at the location you find it.

_____

_____

_____

_____

_____

WHICH WAY IS UP?

Materials: copies of pages 53–54, five bean seeds, double layer of thick paper towels, jar, 8½" x 11" sheet of aluminum foil, water, masking tape

Preparation: Soak the seeds in water for 24 hours before this activity.

Exploration: Ask students to use words and pictures to describe how a seed grows. Explain to the class that plants have a particular motion in response to certain conditions or stimuli. This is called a *tropism.* Moving or growing toward the stimulus is called a *positive tropism.* Moving or growing away from the stimulus is a *negative tropism.* Plants possess tropisms in response to water, gravity, light, dark, and touch. Ask students to draw pictures of a plant in a dark room with a light in a far window. Ask them to draw the plant's response to light. (*The plant should be growing toward the light.*) Tell students they are going to see how a plant responds to gravity.

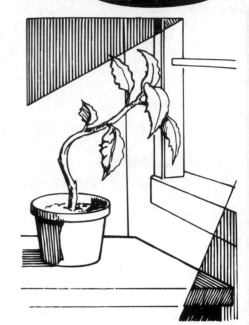

The paper towels will be moistened until soaked, but not dripping. The bean seeds will be placed on the towels and the towels will be rolled. The foil will be folded and crimped around the rolled towels. The paper towel/foil pack will be placed upright in the jar. The top half will be marked with a label that says *UP.* The jar will be placed in an area that will allow the seeds to germinate. After five days, the groups will carefully check inside the towels, without moving the seeds, and draw the growth of the beans on their record sheets. The paper towels will be moistened again and the paper towel/foil pack rolled and covered as before. The pack will be placed upside down in the jar so that the end labeled *UP* will be at the bottom. After waiting another five days and carefully opening the pack, students will observe and draw the beans' growth pattern.

Discovery: When the seed germinates, the root grows downward, regardless of which way the seed is planted. This is *positive geotropism* toward gravity. The stem will turn away from gravity—an example of *negative geotropism.* When the packet is turned over, the roots will change direction to grow downward and the stem will change direction to grow upward. The stem and roots react in this way because of plant growth hormones called *auxins.* Gravity causes auxins to go to one side of the stem or root. The result is the plant curving upward or downward, depending on the part of the plant. Experiments in space are being done to study the effects of low gravity on plants.

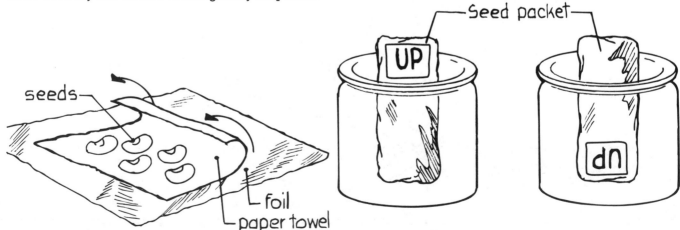

seeds

foil
paper towel

Seed packet

UP

dn

FS-23214 Science Made Simple ■ © Frank Schaffer Publications, Inc.

Which Way Is Up?

Question:
What will be a seed's response when growing upside down?

Prediction:
On your record sheet, draw what a young plant's growth will
look like after being turned upside down and left for a week.

Materials:
five bean seeds
two thick paper towels
jar
8½" x 11" sheet of aluminum foil
water

Procedure and Results:

1. Moisten the double layer of paper towels.

2. Arrange the bean seeds on the paper towels and roll the towels up tightly. Fold the foil around the roll and crimp the edges.

3. Put the seed packet upright in the jar and attach a label marked *UP* to the top end of the packet. Do not disturb for five days.

4. Open the roll carefully. Observe and draw the beans' growth pattern on your record sheet. Roll the paper towels again, moisten carefully, and reseal the roll in the foil.

5. Turn the seed packet upside down in the jar so that the label *UP* is now at the bottom of the jar.

6. After another five days, reexamine the seeds and draw the beans' new growth pattern on your record sheet.

Conclusions:
Answer the following questions on your record sheet:

Do the parts of a plant respond the same to the pull of gravity? Explain using your results.

How would you expect plants to grow in places where gravity is very low? Draw what the plant's growth would look like.

Name _____

Which Way Is Up?

Question:
What will be a seed's response when growing upside down?

Prediction:
Draw what a young plant's growth will look like after being turned upside down and left for a week.

Results:
Show the beans' growth patterns below.

Beans seeds after 5 days

Bean seeds after 10 days

Conclusions:
Do the parts of a plant respond the same to the pull of gravity? Explain using your

results. _____

_____

Draw what a plant's growth would look like in a place where gravity is very low.

SIMPLY MARBLEOUS

Materials: copies of pages 56–58, two large paper clips, two large rubber bands, large book with string tied around it, ruler, 10 marbles

Exploration: Ask a student to demonstrate moonwalking with his or her shoes on. Ask the same child to try it again, this time wearing only socks. Ask the class why it was easier the second time. (*Some students may say the shoes caused the students to "stick." Other students may use the word friction.*) Ask students to rub their hands together briskly. Ask them how it felt. (*Hot*) Explain to the class that this is due to the force of friction. *Friction* is a force between two surfaces that opposes motion and slows moving objects down. Put hand lotion on several students and have them rub their hands together again. Can they get them as hot as before? (*No.*)

Show your students how to assemble the force meter as shown on page 56 using bent paper clips and rubber bands. They need to measure the length of the first rubber band unstretched. After attaching one paper clip to the string and placing the ruler between the two paper clips, they will measure how long the rubber band stretches when a book, with a string around it, is pulled along a surface. They will repeat the experiment placing the book on the 10 marbles. Suggest that children try this on different surfaces to see the difference in force needed to move the book without the marbles.

Discovery: Smooth surfaces reduce friction. Wheels and lubricants can be used to overcome friction. Ball bearings are used to reduce friction. If friction is reduced, then less force is needed to push or pull an object.

BULLETIN BOARD ON FORCES

Have students collect pictures that show friction, gravity, electricity, and magnetism. Arrange the pictures under the correct headings.

Simply Marbleous

Question:
How is a force meter affected by friction reduction?

Prediction:
How will the use of bearings change the force needed to pull a book? Write your prediction on your record sheet.

Materials:
two large paper clips
two large rubber bands
large book with string tied around it
ruler
10 marbles

paper clip   rubber band   paper clip   rubber band

Procedure:
1. Bend the paper clips and assemble the force meter as shown.
2. Measure the length of the first rubber band unstretched.
3. Pull the book along a surface using the force meter attached to the string. Keeping the ruler against the rubber band, measure how far the rubber band stretches when moving the book along the surface.
4. Place the book on the marbles and pull the book again. Measure how long the rubber band stretches when using the marbles.
5. Now try moving the book along a smoother surface and a rougher surface and test the force needed to move the book using the force meter again.

Results:
Observe and measure the amount the rubber band stretched after each trial. Write your measurements on your record sheet.

Conclusions:
Answer the following questions on your record sheet:
What is the effect of using the marbles? How could you use this information to reduce work at home?

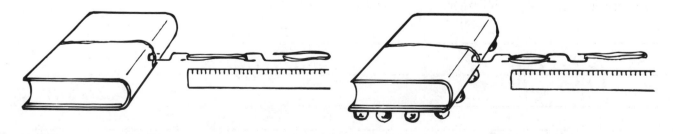

FS-23214 Science Made Simple ■ © Frank Schaffer Publications, Inc.

$\int$imply $\mathbf{M}$arbleous

Question:
How is a force meter affected by friction reduction?

Prediction:
How will the use of bearings change the force needed to pull a book?

_____

_____

Results:
What is the amount the rubber band stretched after each trial?

Type of Surface	Unstretched	No Marbles	With Marbles

Conclusions:
What is the effect of using the marbles?_____

_____

How could you use this information to reduce work at home?_____

_____

_____

_____

INCLINED PLANES

Draw a picture of a barrel on the blackboard. Tell students that the barrel weighs 100 pounds. Ask students to write or draw on a sheet of paper how they could get the barrel six feet off the ground and onto a truck using only one item. (*Most students will choose a rope and describe how they would pull the barrel up.*) Draw a board and show how you would roll the barrel up the board. Explain that the board is a simple machine called an *inclined plane*. Tell the class that a *simple machine* is a tool with one or two parts that changes the force we exert when doing work to make the task easier.

Materials: copies of pages 59–60, eight thick books, board that can act as a ramp, a large rubber band, two large paper clips, ruler, large stapler with string attached, force meter

Exploration: Students will use the force meter they constructed for *Simply Marbleous*. The length of the rubber band will be measured before it is stretched. Groups will attach the force meter to the stapler and lift it straight up. The length the rubber band stretches will be measured. Pulling the stapler up the ramp using the force meter, the children will discover the force reduction of the inclined plane by measuring how far the rubber band now stretches. They will then make the ramp steeper and then more gradually sloped to find out why ramps are usually sloped gently.

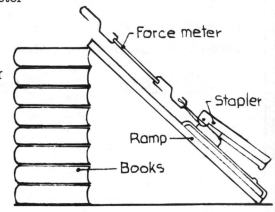

Discovery: It is easier and takes less force to use an inclined plane than lifting something directly against gravity. You exert less force at any one time on a long slope than on a short one. The longer an inclined plane is in relation to its height, the larger the mechanical advantage is.

MATH EXTENSION

Have students build and launch model rockets. Teacher kits for beginners are available from Estee Rockets and can be ordered at hobby stores. Students will use math in measuring as they build the rockets. As they launch their rockets, they can make a simple altimeter and use angles to figure out how high their rockets went. Local rocketry clubs can help.

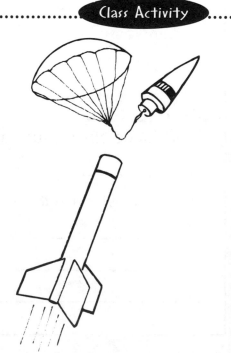

FS-23214 Science Made Simple ■ © Frank Schaffer Publications, Inc.

Inclined Planes

Question:
How do inclined planes help us?

Prediction:
Which inclined plane makes you exert less force, a long
one or a short one? Write your prediction on your record sheet.

Materials:
eight thick books
board that can act as a ramp
large rubber band
two large paper clips
ruler
large stapler with string attached
force meter

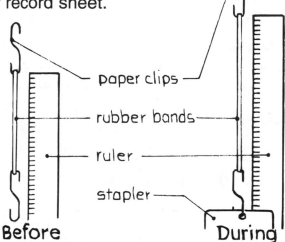

Procedure:
1. Assemble the force meter as shown.
2. Measure the length of the unstretched rubber band.
3. Lift the stapler straight up and measure the length that the rubber band stretches.
4. Put the board on a stack of five books and pull the stapler up the ramp using the force meter. Measure how far the rubber band stretches.
5. Add three books to the stack to make the ramp steeper. Measure the rubber band as you pull the stapler up the ramp.
6. Remove five books from the stack to make the slope gentler. Measure the rubber band as you pull the stapler up the ramp.

Results:
Observe and fill out the data table on your record sheet with your measurements.

Conclusion:
Answer the following questions on your record sheet:

Which ramp took less force?

Why do roads going up a mountain weave back and forth rather than go straight up?

Inclined Planes

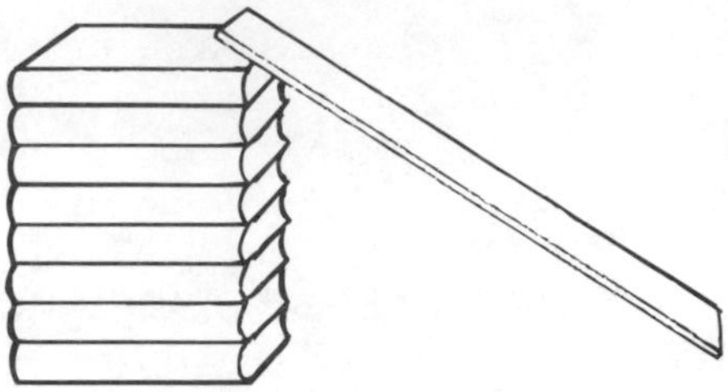

Question:
How do inclined planes help us?

Prediction:
Which inclined plane makes you exert less force, a long one or a short one?

_____

Results:
Observe and fill out the data table with your measurements.

Object	Measurement in Inches
rubber band not stretched	
rubber band pulling stapler straight up	
rubber band using ramp	
rubber band using steeper ramp	
rubber band using gradual slope	

Conclusions:
Which ramp took less force? _____

_____

Why do roads going up a mountain weave back and forth rather than go straight up?

_____

_____

_____

FS-23214 Science Made Simple ▪ © Frank Schaffer Publications, Inc.

RIGHT ON TARGET

Materials: copies of pages 62–63, sock filled with dried pinto beans, book

Exploration: Show your students a sock that is filled with pinto beans and tied with a knot. Explain that they are going to try to drop the sock onto a target while running as fast as they can. Place a book on the ground as a target. Starting about 50 yards from the target, one child will run forward holding the sock at waist level. Then, without stopping, the child will drop the sock as soon as the sock is above the book. Challenge groups to get the sock on the target and not stop running.

Discovery: The sock is a projectile and is moving forward at the same speed as the runner. When the sock is released, it will move forward and downward. The runner provided the forward force and gravity provided the downward force. The path the sock followed was a curved path. By releasing the sock earlier or slowing down, the children can hit the target.

MAKE IT MOVE

Materials: plastic cup, 8½" x 11" sheet of smooth paper, flat table or desk

Exploration: Have the students place a sheet of paper on the edge of the table or desk so that half of it hangs over the edge. Then have them place the cup on the paper on the table. Ask your students what they think will happen if they pull the piece of paper from under the cup. Students will probably think that the cup will fall. Let your students stand at the edge of the table and quickly pull the paper toward them to find out what will happen.

Discovery: The cup will remain on the table because objects at rest will stay at rest unless acted upon by an outside force.

Right on Target

Question:
How will an object fall when dropped by a running student?

Prediction:
If you run with a sock filled with pinto beans and drop it on a target, how many paces from the target will your sock land? Write your prediction on your record sheet.

Materials:
sock filled with dried pinto beans
book

Prediction:
If you run with a sock filled with pinto beans and drop it on a target, how many paces from the target will your sock land? Write your prediction on your record sheet.

Procedure:
1. Tie a knot at the top of the sock filled with pinto beans.
2. Place the book on the floor. The book will be your target.
3. Starting 50 yards from the target, run forward at a rapid speed. Keep the sock waist high.
4. When you get above the target, and without slowing down, release the sock.
5. Measure how many paces from the book your sock landed.
6. Do this two more times, adjusting your speed—faster and slower—to see how your accuracy is affected.
7. Observe one of your classmates trying to hit the target.

Results:
Record the results of your trials on your record sheet. Draw a picture of one of your classmates trying to hit the target.

Conclusion:
Answer the following question on your record sheet.
Besides changing speed, how else could you improve your accuracy?

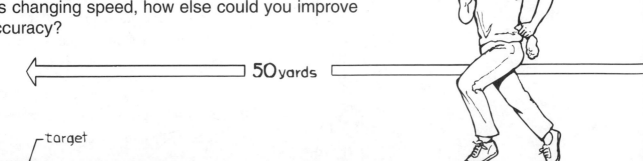

50 yards

target

Right on Target

Question:
How will an object fall when dropped by a running student?

Prediction:
If you run with a sock filled with pinto beans and drop it on a target, how many paces

from the target will your sock land? _____

_____

Results:
Record the results of your trials below.
How many paces from the target did the sock land the first time you attempted the drop?

_____

After running faster, how many paces from the target did the sock land? _____

_____

After running slower, how many paces from the target did the sock land? _____

_____

Draw a picture of one of your classmates trying to hit the target.

_____

Conclusion:
Besides changing speed, how else could you improve your accuracy? _____

_____

Earth Science

Many children live within a few hundred miles of an ocean and yet know very little about the marine environment. But when given an opportunity to consider the ocean, students are soon brimming with questions: "What makes the waves?" "Why is the ocean salty?" "What lives in the ocean?" Modern-day photos taken of Earth from outer space show it to be a blue planet. In fact, over 70 percent of the Earth is covered by water. We know that oceans are important to our survival, as well as the survival of all the Earth's plants and animals. As children learn more about the oceans and come to understand them, the more they will care for them and will want to work hard to protect them from pollution and destruction.

CONCEPTS

The ideas and activities in this section will help children explore the following concepts:

- Temperature and salinity can be a cause of ocean currents.

- The ocean's high salt content is caused by rainwater dissolving the salt in rocks and soil, and rivers carrying this salt to the sea.

- It is easier to float in salt water than fresh water because salty water is denser and, therefore, more buoyant.

LITERATURE RESOURCES

These books are recommended as resources to help students learn about the oceans.

The Magic School Bus on the Ocean Floor by Joanna Cole (Scholastic, 1992). Join Ms. Frizzle and her class as they take a field trip to the bottom of the ocean.

Under the Sea by Frank Talbort (Time-Life, 1995). Illustrations, photographs, and lively text encourage the reader to discover the oceans. This book is part of the Discoveries Library series.

Ocean by Miranda MacQuitty (Knopf, 1995). Colorful photographs show all aspects of the world's oceans. Part of the Eyewitness Books series.

Coral Reef by Barbara Taylor (Dorling Kindersley, 1992). Take an up-close look at the coral reef through larger-than-life photographs. Also in the Look Closer series are *Tide Pool* and *Shoreline*.

I Can Be an Oceanographer by Paul Sipiera (Childrens Press, 1987). In easy-to-understand terms, the author discusses the work oceanographers do as they study the ocean's depths.

Strange Animals of the Sea (National Geographic, 1987). The animals of the ocean pop up for a three-dimensional effect in this National Geographic Action Book.

A House for Hermit Crab by Eric Carle. (Picture Book Studio, 1991). Using colorful illustrations, the author follows Hermit Crab in his search for a new home.

FS-23214 Science Made Simple ■ © Frank Schaffer Publications, Inc.

Ocean Currents

Tell your students that they are going to study some of the reasons for ocean currents. Ask someone to describe what a current is. (*Currents are masses of water that flow in a definite direction.*) Explain that there are two main kinds of currents. The best known are the *surface currents* that are wind-caused. These can be demonstrated by asking the class to blow with straws across a large flat pan of water. Currents can also flow deep below the surface. These are called *deep currents*. The following activities will allow children to explore two of the factors that cause deep currents.

TEMPERATURE CURRENTS

Group Experiment

Tell your class that cold water, like cold air, sinks because it is denser than when it was warm. As cold water sinks, warmer water rises to the surface. This occurs in areas of the world where the water is very cold. The following activity will show how this works in the ocean.

Caution: This activity involves food coloring, so students need to be advised of the possibility of staining clothes. Since it is almost impossible to do this without spillage, it is advised that this activity be done in a large flat-bottomed salad/wash bowl, over a sink, or outside.

Materials: copies of pages 66–67, two 2-liter bottles, hot water (not boiling), ice cold water, food coloring, two index cards, large bowl or sink, colored pencils

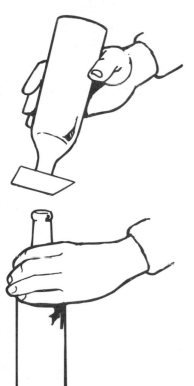

Exploration: Each group will fill one bottle half full with cold water and add seven drops of food coloring to it. The other bottle will be half filled with hot water and no food coloring will be added to it. Your students will place an index card over the colored water bottle and turn it upside down. They should hold the card in place as they slowly turn the bottle over. As the students gently remove their hands, upward air pressure will hold the card in place. Centering the top colored bottle over the mouth of the upright clear bottle, and working over a bowl or sink to catch spills, they will gently slide the card from between the bottles and watch what happens. This experiment will be repeated, but the second time, the hot water is colored and the hot water is placed on top and the cold clear water is on the bottom. Before doing the experiment again, predictions will be made on the record sheet.

Discovery: The first time, the colored cold water sinks to the bottom because it is more dense. Cold water is more dense because it has more mass in a certain volume than warm water. This is because the molecules in warm water are farther apart than the molecules in cold water. The second time, the colored hot water stays on top and the clear cold water stays on the bottom. In most of the world's oceans, the warm, less dense layer of water floats above the colder, more dense bottom layer of water.

Temperature Currents

Question:
How does temperature affect water's movement in the ocean?

Prediction:
Predict what will happen if you fill one bottle half full with hot water and one bottle half full with cold water and put the bottle openings together. What will happen when cold water is on the top? What will happen when hot water is on the top? Draw your predictions on your record sheet.

Materials:

two 2-liter bottles   two index cards
hot water (not boiling)   large bowl or sink
ice cold water   colored pencils
food coloring

Procedure:
1. Fill one bottle half full with ice cold water and add seven drops of food coloring. Mix so that the color is evenly spread throughout the bottle.
2. Fill the other bottle half full with hot clear water.
3. Place the index card over the colored cold water, holding it in place. Slowly turn the bottle over and gently remove your hand. Air pressure will hold the card in place.
4. Center the colored cold water bottle over the clear hot water bottle. Slowly remove the card without disturbing the bottles. Watch what happens.
5. Repeat the experiment by putting colored hot water on top and clear cold water on the bottom. Watch what happens.

Results:
Draw what happened on your record sheet.

Conclusion:
Answer the following question on your record sheet: Where in the oceans might cold water be over warmer water?

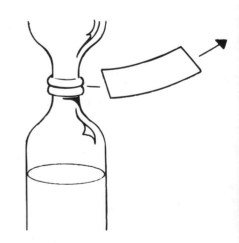

Temperature Currents

Question:
How does temperature affect water's movement in the ocean?

Prediction:
Predict what will happen if you half fill one bottle with hot water and one bottle with cold water and put the bottle openings together. What will happen when cold water is on the top? What will happen when hot water is on the top? Draw your predictions below.

Results:
Draw what actually happened below.

Conclusion:
Where in the oceans might cold water be over warmer water? _____

_____

SALINITY CURRENTS

Tell your class that the ocean is salty because of the salts that are dissolved in water as rainfall runs over rocks and minerals. Eventually the rivers carry dissolved salts into the oceans. The following activity will show how salinity affects deep sea currents.

Caution: This activity involves food coloring, so students need to be advised of the possibility of staining clothes. Since it is almost impossible to do this without spillage, it is advised that this activity be done in a large flat-bottomed salad/wash bowl, over a sink, or outside.

Materials: (per group) copies of pages 69–70, two 2-liter bottles, saltwater solution, tap water, food coloring, two index cards, large bowl or sink, colored pencils

Preparation: You will need to make several gallons of salt water. Mix two tablespoons of kosher or canning salt per quart of water. Large empty plastic water jugs are suggested to accomplish this.

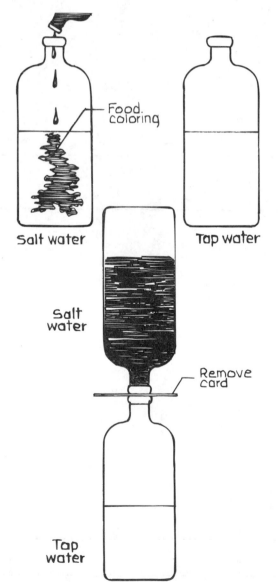

Food coloring

Salt water

Tap water

Salt water

Remove card

Tap water

Exploration: The students will fill one bottle half full with salt water and add seven drops of food coloring to it. The other bottle will be filled half full with tap water and no food coloring will be added to it. Students will place an index card over the colored water bottle and turn it upside down. They should hold the card in place as they slowly turn the bottle over. As they gently remove their hands, upward air pressure will hold the card in place. Centering the top colored bottle over the mouth of the upright clear bottle, and working over a bowl or sink to catch spills, they will gently slide the card from between the bottles and watch what happens. This experiment will be repeated, but the second time, the tap water is colored and is placed on top, and the clear salt water is on the bottom.

Discovery: The first time, the colored salt water will sink to the bottom because it is more dense. The second time, the colored tap water will stay on top and the clear salt water will stay on the bottom. This occurs in Antarctica, where, as ice forms, the top water becomes saltier and sinks to the bottom. Where rivers run into the ocean, fresh water flows over seawater.

∫alinity Currents

Question:
What is the effect of salt on the water in the ocean?

Prediction:
Predict what will happen if you fill one bottle half full with salt water and one bottle half full with tap water and put the bottle openings together. What will happen when salt water is on the top? What will happen when tap water is on the top? Draw your predictions on your record sheet.

Materials:
two 2-liter bottles
saltwater solution
tap water
food coloring
two index cards
large bowl or sink
colored pencils

Procedure:
1. Fill one bottle half full with salt water and add seven drops of food coloring. Mix so that the color is evenly spread throughout the bottle.
2. Fill the other bottle half full with clear tap water.
3. Place the index card over the colored salt water, holding it in place. Slowly turn the bottle over and gently remove your hand. Air pressure will hold the card in place.
4. Center the colored saltwater bottle over the clear tap water bottle. Slowly remove the card without disturbing the bottles. Watch what happens.
5. Repeat the experiment, putting colored tap water on top and clear salt water on the bottom. Watch what happens.

Results:
Draw what happened on your record sheet.

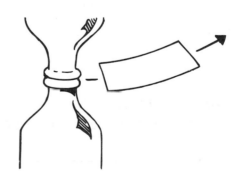

Conclusion:
Answer the following questions on your record sheet:
Where rivers run into the ocean, will the fresh water flow above or below the seawater?
Why?

$\int$alinity Currents

Question:
What is the effect of salt on the water in the ocean?

Prediction:
Predict what will happen if you fill one bottle with salt water and one bottle with tap water and put the bottle openings together. What will happen when salt water is on the top? What will happen when tap water is on the top. Draw your predictions below.

Results:
Draw what happened.

Conclusion:
Where rivers run into the ocean, will the fresh water flow above or below the seawater?

Why? _____

_____

FS-23214 Science Made Simple ■ © Frank Schaffer Publications, Inc.

MAKING A HYDROMETER

Materials: copies of pages 71–72, new pencil with eraser, tap water, three teaspoons salt, teaspoon, three test tubes, thumbtack, permanent marker, jar, ruler

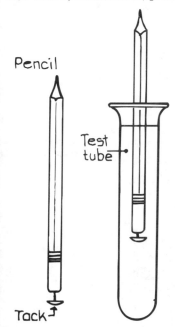

Pencil

Test tube

Tack

Exploration: Ask your class if anyone has ever gone swimming in a saltwater lake or the ocean. Ask the children who have if they tried to float on their backs. Tell the class that floating is another word for *buoyancy.* Float a cork or a piece of paper on a pan of water. Explain to students that buoyancy is an upward force exerted on a floating object by a liquid. Tell students that they are going to see the effect that adding salt to water has on the buoyancy of the water.

Ask each group to make a *hydrometer* by placing a thumbtack at the end of a pencil with a new eraser. Water will be added to three test tubes until the level is one inch below the top. The hydrometer will be floated in the first test tube to note the height it will float without salt. To each of the other test tubes, one and two teaspoons of salt will be added respectively. The solution with the highest density will float the hydrometer the highest.

Discovery: The water with the most salt has the highest density and is the most buoyant.

MATH EXTENSION

The ocean is made of many kinds of salt.
Have students use the data to make a bar or circle graph.

Calcium	1.19%
Magnesium	3.72%
Sodium	30.53%
Potassium	1.11%
Bicarbonate	0.42%
Sulfur	7.67%
Chloride	55.16%
Bromide	0.20%
Total	**100%**

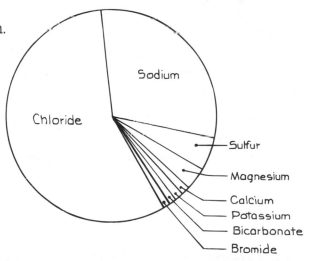

FAMOUS OCEANOGRAPHERS

Have your students research the following famous oceanographers:

Jacques Cousteau—Known for his television shows and books, this famous French scientist dramatized the importance of conserving ocean life.

Dr. Robert Ballard—This famous scientist found the wreck of the sunken Titanic. He enables classes around the world to participate in global explorations through advanced interactive telecommunications.

Jacques Piccard—This Swiss scientist made the deepest dive in a submersible—35,800 feet!

Making a **H**ydrometer

Question:
A hydrometer measures the density of a liquid. How will adding salt to water change the reading on a thermometer?

Prediction:
Which solution—plain water, water with a little salt, or water with more salt—will cause the hydrometer to float the highest? Write your prediction on your record sheet.

Materials:
new pencil with eraser
tap water
three teaspoons of salt
teaspoon
three test tubes
thumbtack
permanent marker
jar
ruler

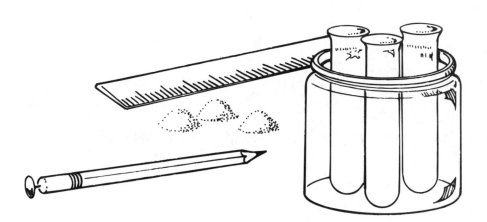

Procedure:
1. Place the thumbtack in the eraser end of the pencil.
2. Fill each test tube with tap water up to one inch from the top. Store the test tubes in the jar.
3. Float the pencil in one test tube. Mark the water level on the pencil using the permanent marker.
4. Add one teaspoon of salt to another test tube. Mix using your thumb to cover the test tube.
5. Repeat using two teaspoons of salt.

Results:
Observe each test tube. Measure the distance from the eraser to the mark for each solution. Write your results on your record sheet.

Conclusion:
Pretend that a ship is loaded with cargo. Using the findings from above, draw the ship floating in the ocean and the ship floating in a freshwater lake on your record sheet.

Making a Hydrometer

Question:
A hydrometer measures the density of a liquid. How will adding salt to water change the reading on a thermometer?

Prediction:
Which solution—plain water, water with a little salt, or water with more salt—will cause the hydrometer to float the highest?

Results:
Observe each test tube. Measure the distance from the eraser to the mark for each solution. Write your results below.

Test Tube Contents	Distance From Eraser
tap water	
tap water and 1 teaspoon salt	
tap water and 2 teaspoons salt	

Conclusion:
Pretend that a ship is loaded with cargo. Using the findings from above, draw the ship floating in the ocean and the ship floating in a freshwater lake.

Ship in Ocean	Ship in Lake

THE SALTY OCEAN

Materials: paper cup, plastic spoon, coffee filter, funnel, jar, table salt, soil, water, dark-colored saucer or plastic party plate

Exploration: The ocean is an important source of food, energy, and minerals. The waters of the ocean contain every natural element. But the one element the ocean is most known for is salt. Almost four percent of the ocean is made up of different kinds of salts. Ninety-nine percent of the ocean's salinity is made up of the following six elements: chloride, sodium, sulfur, magnesium, calcium, and potassium. Sodium chloride, or ordinary table salt, is the dominant salt compound in the ocean. But where did all this salt come from and how did it get in the ocean? Most of the salt in the ocean comes primarily from the erosion of rocks and soil by rainwater. After the salts are removed from the soil and rocks by the beating rain, they are swept into rivers that carry them into the ocean. Volcanoes and undersea springs also send salts to the ocean.

Separate students into groups of three or four. Have students mix the soil and the salt together. Tell each group to place the coffee filter in the funnel and spoon the soil-and-salt mixture into the filter. Have students place their funnels in their jars and pour one-third cup of water through the soil-and-salt mixture into the jars. When the water has stopped dripping, tell students to remove the funnel and pour the water from each jar onto a plate. Have students set the plates in the sunlight so that the water will evaporate. When the water has evaporated, students will see salt crystals that have been left behind.

WHERE IN THE WORLD?

Have each student bring in a newspaper or magazine article about an event that mentions the ocean—hurricanes, typhoons and other storms, tsunamis, oil spills and other pollution problems, ocean animal locations, etc. Put these articles on a bulletin board near a world map. Have each child find the ocean where his or her event took place.

Art Project

Art Extensions

The ocean is the home of many different environments such as coral reefs, tide pools, kelp forests, and the deep ocean bottom. Have students pick one of the areas, research it, and make a small pop-up book about that habitat.

Technology in the Classroom

INSTRUCTIONAL TELEVISION (ITV)

Instructional television provides many benefits to teachers and students. It expands the viewers' world, clarifies specific points, enriches the curriculum, engages attention, summarizes or reviews information, simplifies and reinforces concepts, and motivates students to learn. Instructional television segments serve to complement the lesson for a teacher and should be shown in conjunction with an activity or lesson. Consult your local school district to find out how to access ITV in your community. *Cable in the Classroom*, provided by many local cable stations, has a schedule of some of the ITV programs available in your area as well as suggested classroom lessons.

Bill Nye the Science Guy—This series combines science with music, video, graphics, special effects, and comedy. (Grades 4–6; 30 minutes each)

Eureka—This series features basic concepts of physics using cartoon characters and animated objects. (Grade 5+; 30 programs at 5 minutes each)

Science Is Elementary—This series has an exploration section illustrating examples of the topic, concept development of the principle being studied, and an application segment showing real-world situations. (Grades K–4; 10 programs at 15 minutes each)

Take a Look—This is an environmental studies series showing the role of science in our daily lives. Experiments are also suggested. (Grades 2–4; 20 programs at 10 minutes each)

Up Close and Natural—This series examines a wide variety of animals and explores their habitats. (Grade 4+; 15 programs at 15 minutes each)

The Magic School Bus—Based on the popular book by Joanna Cole, this animated series shows Ms. Frizzle and her class taking field trips into the body, out into space, and many other places, where they explore scientific principles. (Grades 1–4; 30 minutes each)

3-2-1 Classroom Contact—This series actively engages students in all aspects of science using live-action, music, animation, and on-location interviews. (Grades 4–6; 30 programs at 15 minutes each)

A Home for Pearl—This series teaches students about animal habitats. (Grades K–5; 4 programs at 20 minutes each)

WHERE ON THE WEB?

Search the following World Wide Web sites to find out more about science.

General Science

Bill Nye
http://nyelabs.kcts.org

Life Science

The Oceania Project
http://www.nor.com.au/users/oceania/

WhaleNet
http://whale.wheelock.edu

E-Patrol
http://www.sprint.com/epatrol/

National Wildlife Federation
http://www.nwf.org/nwf/kids/index.html

Project Wild
http://www.nceet.snre.umich.edu/wild/guides.html

Earth Science

Smithsonian Ocean Planet
http://seawifs.gsfc.nasa.gov/OCEAN_PLANET/
HTML/ocean_planet_topic_outline.html

Captain Planet
http://www.turner.com/planet/index.html

Mission to Planet Earth
http://www.hq.nasa.gov/office/mtpe/science.html

Physical Science

Exploratorium
http://www.exploratorium.edu/

FS-23214 Science Made Simple • © Frank Schaffer Publications, Inc.

Answer Key

Answers may vary. Accept reasonable answers.

Page 5—The Powers of Observation
Conclusion: Numerical data is far more reliable and easier to share with other scientists.

Page 11 Food Webs
Results: **crab**–consumer, decomposer; **phytoplankton**–producer; **sperm whale**–consumer, predator; **anchovy**–consumer, predator, prey; **flying fish**–consumer, predator, prey; **killer whale**–consumer, predator; **dolphin**–consumer, predator, prey; **shark**–consumer, predator; **zooplankton**–consumer, prey; **squid**–consumer, predator, prey; **tuna**–consumer, predator, prey; **seabird**–consumer, predator, prey; **salmon**–consumer, predator, prey; **blue whale**–consumer, predator, prey; **hatchetfish**–consumer, predator, prey

Conclusions: If the phytoplankton were killed and the phytoplankton was at the bottom of the food chain, all animals would eventually die.
If the anchovies moved to warmer water, the tuna would follow. The local fishermen would be left without tuna to catch or have to travel great distances in order to fish.

Page 19—Food Pyramids
Results: Answers will vary. One possible answer:
Fourth-level Consumer: killer whale
Third-level Consumer: blue whale
Second-level Consumer: anchovy
First-level Consumer: zooplankton
Producers: phytoplankton
The population of first-level consumers is the largest.

Conclusion: The larger animals are usually at the top of the food pyramid. The smaller animals are at the bottom of the pyramid.

Page 23—Climates
Results: Answers will vary.

Conclusions: Overall, the temperature should be cooler at the bottom. The lowest temperatures should be under the soil or in the shade. The highest temperatures should be on the playground or in the sand.

Page 26—Decomposers
Results: Answers will vary.

Conclusion: Since fungus aids in the decomposition of dead material, and death is a natural end of life for living things, then dead things would start to accumulate greatly if there was nothing to aid in their decomposition.

Page 29—Landfills
Results: The fruit will decompose. Most items will show little decomposition.

Conclusion: Answers will vary.

Page 33—What Color Is Black?
Results: Answers will vary depending on the colors used.

Conclusion: This is an example of a physical change since the colors were being separated, but not changed.

Page 36—Rust
Results: Measurements will vary.

The vinegar soaked wad had rust.
The dry wad had a coating on it to prevent rust from forming easily.

Conclusions: Rust, or iron oxide, formed in the tube that had the treated wad of steel wool.
As oxygen was used up in the tube with the vinegar-soaked wad, water rose in the tube to fill the space of the oxygen.

Page 38—That's a Gas!
Results: Bubbles were produced and a noise could be heard when the seltzer tablets were added.
The lighted match was extinguished when put in the gas produced by the seltzer tablet.

Conclusions: This experiment is an example of a chemical change because new products were produced. Since the flame was extinguished, oxygen could not be the gas. The gas produced was carbon dioxide. Carbon dioxide is frequently used in fire extinguishers.

Page 41—Which Dough Will Grow?
Results: Answers will vary.

Conclusions: The higher temperatures increase the rate of fermentation of the yeast and increase the production of carbon dioxide. The bread will rise higher. Lower temperatures slows the rate of fermentation. The bread will not rise as high. Very low temperatures will not allow the chemical reaction to proceed. The bread should not rise.
Bakers wait before putting bread in the oven to allow the bread to rise. Otherwise the bread will be flat.

© FS-23214 Science Made Simple ▪ © Frank Schaffer Publications, Inc.

Page 44—The Gas We Breathe
Results: Students will see many bubbles being produced and rising to the surface. The water level will go down on the inverted test tube.

Conclusions: The glowing splint burst into flames because the gas is oxygen.
Animals in the ocean need oxygen. Green plants such as elodea produce oxygen. Many animals have adaptations that allow them to "breathe" while under the water. Other animals must come to the surface in order to breathe.

Page 47—The Amazing Falling Cup
Results: The water came out of the hole in a steady stream when the cup was held the first time.
When the cup was dropped, the water stopped coming out of the hole.

Conclusions: Gravity was the force acting on the water the first time.
The second time gravity was acting on the cup and the water.
The water and the cup fell at the same rate, so water did not come out of the hole. This condition is called microgravity.

Page 51—Center of Gravity
Conclusions: The center of gravity is not always in the center of an object.
Answers vary.

Page 54—Which Way Is Up?
Conclusions: The parts of a plant do not respond the same to the pull of gravity. Roots grow toward gravity and bend when the seed is turned around in order to grow down. Stems grow against gravity and the stem bends in order to grow up. In microgravity, a plant's growth would not be affected by gravity. Light and water would have a stronger determination over the direction that the plant grows. Stems grow toward light. Roots grow toward water. The plant might send roots and/or stems off in other directions than up and down.

Page 57—Simply Marbleous
Results: Answers will vary because of the size and thickness of the rubber bands.

Conclusions: The marbles acted like bearings and reduced friction. The marbles have a hard surface and there is less friction. Adding the marbles changed the friction from sliding friction to rolling friction. Reducing the friction made it easier to move.
At home, when moving a heavy object that cannot be lifted, it would be easier to roll it on a dolly or cart than to slide it.

Page 60—Inclined Planes
Results: Answers will vary because of the size of the rubber bands.

Conclusions: The lower-angled ramp will stretch the rubber band less than the steeper ramp.
If roads went straight over a mountain, it would make the engine work too hard. Some cars and trucks can travel straight up a steep slope, but most would overheat. By cutting back and forth, the road can make a more gradual slope and the forces on the car's engine are less over a longer distance.

Page 63—Right on Target
Results: Answers will vary. Students will find that the sock was beyond the target. Running faster made the forward force greater. Running slower put less forward force and the object would be closer.

Conclusion: Besides changing speed, a person could release the sock before the target.

Page 67—Temperature Currents
Results: Cold water sinks the first time. The second time, the hot water stays on the top and the cold water is on the bottom.

Conclusion: In polar regions, the surface water becomes colder and sinks. Warmer water from below then rises to the surface.

Page 70—Salinity Currents
Results: The first time, the colored salt water sank and the tap water rose. The second time, salt water stayed on the bottom with no mixing. The color stayed on the top.

Conclusion: The fresh water will flow above the seawater because salt makes the seawater more dense.

Page 73—Making a Hydrometer
Results: Answers will vary. The distance will be the shortest for the test tube with two teaspoons of salt and the pencil will float the highest.

Conclusion: The ship in the ocean should be higher on the surface of the water than the ship in the freshwater lake.

FS-23214 Science Made Simple ▪ © Frank Schaffer Publications, Inc.